MASTER OF THE ARTS: EXCEL AT SAYING NO

CHANGE THE HABIT OF PLEASING, OVERCOME THE FEAR TO REFUSE, GAIN YOUR TIME AND RESPECT, SAY NO WITHOUT FEELING GUILTY, GROW YOUR WEALTH AND SUCCESS

BEAU YOUNG, PH.D

© **Copyright 2020 - All rights reserved.**

The content contained within this book may not be reproduced, duplicated, or transmitted without direct written permission from the author or the publisher.

Under no circumstances will any blame or legal responsibility be held against the publisher, or author, for any damages, reparation, or monetary loss due to the information contained within this book, either directly or indirectly.

Legal Notice:

This book is copyright protected. It is only for personal use. You cannot amend, distribute, sell, use, quote or paraphrase any part, or the content within this book, without the consent of the author or publisher.

Disclaimer Notice:

Please note the information contained within this document is for educational and entertainment purposes only. All effort has been executed to present accurate, up to date, reliable, complete information. No warranties of any kind are declared or implied. Readers acknowledge that the author is not engaged in the rendering of legal, financial, medical, or professional advice. The content within this book has been derived from various sources. Please consult a licensed professional before attempting any techniques outlined in this book.

By reading this document, the reader agrees that under no circumstances is the author responsible for any losses, direct or indirect, that are incurred as a result of the use of the information contained within this document, including, but not limited to, errors, omissions, or inaccuracies.

CONTENTS

Introduction   5

1. How Much You Sacrifice For Not Saying No   15
2. Why Is it Hard To Say No?   29
3. Mental Preparation For Saying No   46
4. Set Your Boundaries, When To Say No   65
5. The Strategies Of Saying No, What To Say   84
6. How To Deliver The No Message   99
7. The Tactics Of Difficult People And How To Deal With them   107
8. Common Issues To Avoid When Saying No   119
9. Tips To Say No by Scenario   125
10. Your Life with The Power Of Saying No   138

Conclusion   143
References   147

YOUR SUCCESS BOOKLET

(Read this before you start any success journey...)

This booklet includes:

- 9 things that successful people are different from the mediocre
- 15 things successful people say no to
- 8 Steps to achieve anything you want in life

Get yourself mentally equipped before the journey starts.

To receive your success booklet, visit the link:

https://beausuccess.activehosted.com/f/1

INTRODUCTION

Your cellphone alarm wakes you up after not enough sleep. Is it morning already? You bash the annoying alarm off. Time to get up, get dressed, and get ready for work. You don't waste time – the sooner you leave, the better: that darn rush hour traffic! You grab the sandwich you made last night (nifty time-saver!) and munch on it while waiting at the nearest bus stand.

Looking at your brand-new watch, you wonder why on earth you spent so much on a luxury when you knew you shouldn't have.

"This certainly won't sit well with my wife!" you think.

The bus arrives, you climb aboard and find a seat. The rest of the way, you enjoy your sandwich and scroll through your messages. Just before you are about to put the phone away, something catches your eye. It is a message from your co-worker Rick that just popped in, and immediately you know he's asking for a favor.

Rick's text: *Hey Liam! Can you cover for me at the office? I had to drop a friend of mine off late last night, and I never got any sleep. Thanks a bunch! Please also ensure to log me in the system. I owe you one!*

As if the day hadn't started bad enough. Now you need to clean up the mess someone else has made, and lie to cover your co-worker, in case someone inquires about his whereabouts.

The rest of the way, you sit quietly and curse yourself for being such a people-pleaser. You can't say No at home, you can't say No at work, and you most certainly struggle to say No to yourself as well. Such an approach has already caused you lots of problems in life.

"I can't keep living on like this. This has to end!"

You eventually reach the office, quickly sign yourself in and go through your email to ensure you didn't miss anything. Turns out, you have a report due for submission in less than an hour. This report is everything you have been working on, and failure to submit would most likely see you land in a world of trouble.

Still, you have an hour, so you quickly rush to Rick's workstation and log him in. You take a quick look through his to-do list and find out he also has an assignment that is due today. You don't have time to do it – you've got your own work to do. But now Rick is going to be annoyed. And he's going to take that out on you. Right about now, you kick yourself and think, why did I get myself into this mess? Why couldn't I just say No?

Fast forward, you complete your report and submit it on time. Rick, on the other hand, arrives late. He has barely a few minutes before the submission, which leaves him in a bit of a dilemma.

Although Rick appreciates the fact that you logged him in, he is insistent that you could have at least informed him about the due assignment. You feel like you could have done that too, if only you had the time; perhaps you should have said No to begin with.

This all sounds really familiar, does it not? We all have been through such situations where, out of sheer generosity and care, we agree to do someone a small favor numerous times, and yet we get pointed at if things go wrong.

Rick asked you to log him in, and you did. Nowhere in the text did he mention anything about assignments, and even if he had mentioned it, you had your own issues to sort out. Clearly, your good nature brought in nothing but embarrassment and frustration. At this point, you might think that you would never do anything for anyone ever again. Spoiler alert: a few weeks later, you'll still be doing this, if not for Rick, then someone else.

The problem isn't how irresponsible people like Rick are. The real problem lies in how inept people are when it comes to saying No to others or to themselves. Avoiding saying No invites a world of issues, extra work, and shouldering unnecessary burdens. A person may be the brightest mind by a country mile, but their abilities and efforts are all clipped and curbed by these unexpected favors. To add insult to injury, these 'favors' you continue to grant will never pay you back with anything.

This is not the end of it. Many struggles in life, whether personal or professional, can be traced back to the inability to say No. For instance, with overspending. People who work hard and manage to save their finances often find themselves tempted to make extravagant purchases, which they regret buying later on. Those who pursue opportunities let their emotions take over, and agree to do almost anything for the opportunity later regretting making those agreements. Our inability to say No can lead us into consequences we are not ready to face.

Will those who you've helped, help you back? Prepare for disappointment... Ask someone you've helped for ages, without asking for anything in return, to give you a hand. How quickly did their excuses come? What was the excuse? Not feeling well, maybe. Or was it the "I've-got-an-appointment-across-town" one? Regardless of what it was, there is a big chance that they won't help.

If that is the case, why do we continue helping them? Why do we see it as "doing them a favor" when clearly they view it differently; in retrospect the impression they give is they're taking advantage of us. This may sound like a bit of a surprise, but it really is our own fault. There is no denying that we would always seek out easier ways of doing our tasks, even if that means asking for help from those who are willing to offer it. The only difference is that when it comes to us, we just do not know when to stop offering help. This means that we cannot blame anyone else but ourselves for not being able to say, "You know, I am really busy right now." Or "I am really sorry, but I cannot help you."

A simple word, and yet most of us are terrified beyond rational explanation. Honestly, how hard can it be to say No? What is the worst that can happen if we do say No? Yet, we continue to sacrifice ourselves because we think we are making others or ourselves happy; the reality is far from it.

Such people, who are constantly being nice and doing the extra work for others, are often overlooked by society at large.

Bosses, who indeed take note of workers, continue to keep them away from promotions because doing so shows them our greatest weakness: the lack of confidence and assertiveness to say No. It shows that we do not have the authority needed higher up the hierarchy.

It is time to change all that. People need to understand that by not turning down additional work and those never-ending favors, they are exhausting themselves, which takes a toll on their quality of life. Such people are often found in a stressed-out zone with a massive frown on their faces. Additionally, relationships suffer, and that is never good. What people need is some help to allow them to feel empowered and on top of their game.

If you have had enough living such a life, take a deep breath, and promise yourself that you will:

- Do what is needed to learn how to say No
- Never fall for the same traps ever again
- Stand your ground and take control of your life
- Learn what it takes to develop assertiveness
- Change your life
- Lead a better life on your own terms
- Never look back

Let this book guide your self-exploration; let's meet the better person that resides within you. I'll teach you to be the driver instead of being a passenger to take control back. All that you will find here is not just hearsay; everything I share would be backed up by what the experts have already said. Trust yourself and keep telling yourself that you can do this, and I assure you, you will walk out of your home a new person in the next 30 days!

THE READERS

This book aims to provide all the essential information and guidelines to people who find themselves afraid and struggling to say No to their friends, their family members, and co-workers. Whether you are a man who is trying his best to maintain a balance in life and lead a life without sacrificing yourself or a woman who is tired of giving in to requests and being burdened by additional responsibilities at home or work, I aim to show you just how you can come out of this.

While most consider saying No would mean losing the respect of those around us, the reality is quite the opposite. Being assertive and in command is always something the world desires. Learning this takes time, and I urge the readers to continue practicing all that they will discover here. With perseverance and dedication, no obstacle is too big to conquer, and no path is too difficult to walk on.

This book is written with two primary purposes in mind. The first purpose is to help you grow stronger with in-depth mental exercises and information. The second part focuses primarily on the actions which one must take to acquire the desired results.

To make this experience even better, I would recommend noting down important points for quick reference later, so keep a notebook handy for the questions you have or the exercises to do – then you can review them later on.

Who Am I?

It is only fair to know who the author is and what exactly makes them the authority or the right person to teach you all this. Here is a quick introduction about me and what I have done so far that allows me to help you out with your problems.

My name is Beau Young (Ph.D.). Having spent years as a business and personal coach and a consultant as well, I have helped hundreds of individuals and entrepreneurs from all walks of life to achieve the personal happiness and business successes they so desperately sought. Everyone in life has a passion they love to pursue, and mine just happens to be helping people to feel a lot happier and more successful.

When it comes to self-improvement, there is no denying that a significant focus is on how to improve one's level of happiness, and this is where the ability to say No truly shines. It plays one of the most essential roles in increasing our happiness levels by quite some margin. For years, I have researched and tested numerous strategies and helped others apply these strategies to see what the results were.

Master of The Arts: Excel at Saying No is the sharing of my knowledge and experience with the many people who can benefit from it but who I am simply unable to meet face-to-face. Through this book, I intend to show everyone that, contrary to popular belief, it is not hard to say No without ever feeling guilty.

After you have gone through my book and applied the strategies effectively, you will experience a completely new life. You will find yourself more assertive and in control. You will be far more confident than you may be at this point in time, and you will have no problem in saying No to those annoying and frankly frustrating additional burdens, which are not your responsibilities to bear. You might even be surprised to read this, but people will pay more attention to you.

Furthermore, you will lead a life that would be more relaxed, meaning that you would be able to enjoy your life to the fullest and save a significant time that would otherwise be wasted by those additional tasks.

I have had the honor to coach many people who began our journey together with low assertiveness, and every other day I get credited for their success, though the true credit lies with them and their willingness to change. Through my training, people continue to change their lives and lead a happier life for themselves and their loved ones. They are able to maintain excellent relationships and a thriving professional life at the same time. The book comprises exactly the same content, making me ever so confident that you would certainly find the results you desire.

With my help and my expertise, I will ensure that you are fully equipped with the skills, tools, and the knowledge you need to change your current situation and transform yourself into someone who is confident and successful. The best part is, you never have to feel guilty about saying no, ever again.

For far too long, you have already done enough for the world, and that has taken a toll on your life. You have lost precious time in doing things for others, and in due process, you have sidelined your life for the sake of others. You may think you can continue on like this, but the fact is that you may just be on the verge of collapse. Act now, and you would save yourself from disastrous consequences.

Yes, the entire process takes a bit of time to understand and apply in life fully. However, you do not have to wait a year or even half of that; 30 days, and you should see the results forthcoming. Between then and now stand your will and dedication. Muster enough of them to go through the book and learn the secret recipe to success, and before you know it, you would be looking back to this day with no regrets at all.

1

HOW MUCH YOU SACRIFICE FOR NOT SAYING NO

Let's be clear: being helpful is good. Everybody appreciates helpfulness. What we're talking about in this book is balance – out of balance is saying yes to almost all requests (or seen from the other side: not saying no) to the point that you pay for it, to the degree it negatively impacts your life. So before we dive into figuring out how we can learn to say No confidently, we first need to take a step back and understand a few facts. We need to analyze how things are and pay more attention to what price we pay for not saying no.

If you come to think of it, you can lose a lot more than just an argument – you can also lose your finances, your savings, your prestige, your temperament, even your moral compass; the list is too extensive to cover. However, we are here to learn and learn we shall!

> *"Half of the troubles of this life can be traced to saying yes too quickly and not saying no soon enough."*
>
> — JOSH BILLINGS

That is quite a statement, and perhaps a perfect way to begin the first chapter. Brace yourselves as this chapter will not only open your eyes to reality, but it may even make you realize how much you've lost already. By the end of the chapter, however, you will feel better knowing that you can make situations go in your favor instead. A wake-up call, if you wish to call it that, can be a little unexpected and even intimidating, but it is only after waking up that you realize just how much in life you have to live for and are missing out on.

Thus, far in your life, you may have shown yourself as a person who is willing to help others, even if that means sacrificing yourself. Truth be told, that is what separates us from the ones who really succeed in life. I am not saying that such people are selfish. Instead, they find other ways to give back to the community.

> "The difference between successful people and really successful people is that really successful people say no to almost everything."
>
> — WARREN BUFFET

IRREPARABLE LOSSES

Unknown to us, while we are trying to gain someone's trust or keep it, we can lose, and sometimes those losses are life-changingly bad. I can write a complete book on just how much we lose when we are trying to please others and taking on additional responsibilities. These could be friends who are asking you to 'trust' them with your savings or assets. These could be your close family members who ask you to keep the faith and know that they will always do what is best for you. Each one of us has been through such a situation at least once, if not more. Those who ended up suffering now realize just how much things could go wrong: the loss of a perfectly healthy relationship, work jeopardized, and unnecessary issues drawn your way.

Not long ago, a friend of mine experienced a negative life-changing event. Seeing him depressed and hopeless served as a deep lesson for me. Here's what happened: Peter was always looking for ways to maximize his earnings. I don't blame him for looking out for opportunities because we all do that. However, he didn't know he was about to walk into an overwhelming loss.

Mark, a friend of Peter's, approached him and persuaded him to invest in a business venture. The business venture seemed easy and profitable. The entire idea was to buy beer and export it to China, where the demand for US beer was high.

Peter was convinced by Mark to invest $30,000 into the idea. Mark assured Peter that he had everything in order, such as the buyers, distribution channels, and logistics. Both Peter and Mark had been friends for as long as I can remember. Naturally,

Peter trusted Mark, and there had been no reason so far for Peter to think otherwise. Then things started to go wrong.

Peter was asked to invest in the business and let the rest be handled by his friend. The only thing Mark asked in return was not to undergo the contracts or any kind of legal documentation certifying that Peter was going to invest an amount of money into the business. This is where Peter had to make a call. A good business person would normally walk away from such a situation since there is very little information available, especially on the side of distribution channels, but Peter did not. After all, his good friend was on the other end. Peter knew that Mark was undergoing some financial issues, and given the way he portrayed this business idea, this can be the opportunity for both of them to make a good profit, and this means a lot for Mark and his family. Peter dared not imagine how Mark would react if he said no to him.

Peter wanted to help his friend out and maintain the bond of friendship and trust. Asking for paperwork may have put a dent into their friendship, and Peter was not going to let that happen.

The money was then invested in a single tranche. Peter had nothing to worry about since Mark assured him he would take care of everything. It did not take much time for Peter to realize that there was never going to be any sales. Despite constant reassurance from Mark that his contacts would provide the help they needed – upon which Peter agreed to invest – Mark was unable to fetch any help when they really needed it. Not a single case of beer was ever sold. When Peter tried to bring up the issue, Mark would either make excuses and cut the line, or act strangely.

There was a time when Mark and Peter would hang out almost every other day. Now, Mark was nowhere to be seen. Peter's money was invested in acquiring the beers from a brewery, the shipping cost, and everything in the middle. The beer even made it to China, but it never left the warehouse. Although Mark continued to promise that there were significant buyers in China who would buy these cases of beer as soon as they arrived, the reality was anything but that. The beer expired and was eventually counted as a total write-off.

Mark felt embarrassed and ashamed by the huge failure. He was also unable to face his friend, which ultimately led him to move away to a new city. In the end, it was Peter who ended up with both an irreparable financial loss and the loss of a friend.

When I first got to know about this, I was pretty shocked. I knew Peter very well, yet was struggling to make sense of the entire situation – how had he trusted someone so blindly? When I asked him this, he said there were a couple of reasons and, of course, wanting to make a profit is one of them, but the main reason is that he didn't want to disappoint his friend.

He knows now, with the power of hindsight, that all he had to do was to say No. If Mark was truly a friend, he would have continued to remain in touch and hung out with him as usual. Being betrayed by someone close can hurt a lot worse. There are so many examples around the world where people have willingly given in to such exuberant ideas despite the risk to their relationships in the hope of maintaining trust. They soon realize that trust was never really there to begin with.

Saying No is not rude – it's a clear and definitive way to draw a line in the sand; to let others know what you can do and what you can't. Sure, there are things we are comfortable doing, and then there are things which we just don't. These can be perceived as an extra burden, a hateful chore, a boring task, or even a frightening one. Each of our lives is ours to live. We go through our individual choices and bear the consequences on our own. If our lives are the sum of our decisions, why let others force us to do things we don't want to?

By saying yes quickly, not only are you showing yourself as a weaker person, but you are also encouraging others around you to rely on you when things go bad for them, whilst the reverse is almost never true. To some extent, being solid and dependable and reliable is a good thing, just don't do this to the degree that it is to your own detriment or with requests that don't make sense to you. Experiencing doubt? Walk away. If they persist, then at most offer some friendly, valuable advice. And then really walk away.

Just like Peter, you too may find yourself in a similar situation. You too may have a friend like Mark, constantly talking about how you should invest in stocks or a start-up business idea just because they have a hunch. You may listen a few times without saying anything, but there will come the point when you either lose your patience and tell them to stop talking, or actually start searching on your own and find the idea worthwhile. Understand the risks: could the consequences be severe financial losses, the kind that would take ages to recover from.

Apart from financial losses, which somehow can be recovered with time, not saying No can have psychological implications as well. These are the kind of 'side-effects' which can leave you emotionally or psychologically scarred for a considerable time. Take a moment and examine whether they are happening to you right now; you may never have noticed them before. Continue leading the same lifestyle, and the consequences could be anything but bearable.

If the things you say yes to are directly in line with your core values, objectives, and goals, then all should be well, and you might actually enjoy saying yes. On the other hand, if you were saying yes to that which goes against your own moral code, your own core values, then you are walking into a potential disaster.

You always have a choice – your only option isn't just the option suggested. It never is. Pursue what your own heart and mind tell you, even if that means going against the idea pitched by your spouse, your siblings, or even your friends. By continually being the one who says yes to practically everything, with no filters, you'll be the one with a laundry list of problems. Here are some of them to give you a better idea of just how many issues you invite to your life.

Bad Relationships

There is no denying that most relationships, even the healthy ones, go through a phase where a couple argues. It is a natural aspect of life, one that cannot be avoided. The mature thing to do in an argument is to let the other person speak completely and then go on to explain yourself and your situation. However, these days, we immediately start fleeing from the foreseeable issues, and to put an end to the argument, we often cave in, especially the ladies.

Contrary to popular belief, saying yes and being pleasing and helpful does not always support a healthy relationship. To be true to yourself and your partner, you must know what you can and can't do. By submitting to the partner's requests, by immediately saying yes to favors and demands, you are harming your relationship in the long run. Sure, at first, everything would seem to go smoothly. With the passage of time, you will start having second thoughts. Once that happens, you might start feeling manipulated. Consider also that by saying yes every time, you are not being honest with your partner about how you truly feel. You may have even come to a point where you do not know what your real feelings are anymore.

In the simplest words, you would effectively be stuck between two worlds. On the one hand, you feel you are being manipulated by your partner, and arguing about it would certainly not bring out any answers for you. On the other hand, you are not being honest, and you know your partner could very well use this as a counter-argument. In both cases, you have no option but to shut yourself down.

The problem is that these issues carry on even within friends as well. Needless to say, you are risking losing all of it if you continue to sacrifice yourself. At first, saying yes is perceived as a way of assuring the trust between friends, but then again, it is just a perceived image. The reality takes you in the opposite direction. Not only are you hiding your true feelings from your best of friends, but you are also creating doubts in your mind and theirs. As time goes on, you feel like you are not honest with them, that you can't be honest with them, but at the same time, you worry that by doing so, you may ultimately hurt them.

It is likely that by saying yes to everything your friend has to say, they may start doubting that you have any depth to you. It can also go the other way round, and that is where you may feel the other party is using your habit of saying yes for their vested interests, as manipulation.

This would naturally cause issues, bring up heated arguments, and eventually would result in a massive and disappointing fall-out: not something to look forward to.

Lack Of Identity

When others request our help, we can become preoccupied with those requests, spending our time and effort turning *their* dreams into reality whilst losing track of what we really wanted to do for *ourselves*. Our core values and personal goals are what define our identities, and losing sight of these means losing our personal identities.

There comes the point in a person's life where he/she may have no clue what to do and what to expect out of life. They may not be able to recall what they like and what they hate because by then, they would have sacrificed a significant part of their lives trying to make others happy. Once again, the lack of personal identity leads to depression, anxiety, and its tag-along buddy, stress.

Anxiety, Stress, And Depression

According to the Anxiety and Depression Association of America, an alarming 18.1% of the population suffers from anxiety disorders every year. (Facts & Statistics | Anxiety and Depression Association of America, ADAA, n.d.). Anxiety can lead to chaotic results if not kept in check.

Accepting requests from friends, partners, or co-workers has time implications. The limited time you have to pursue your own goals reduces further, and your focus shifts away from your own important tasks. In the process of shuffling priorities, any effective self-managing routines become stretched and inefficient, leading to an increase in anxiety. The combination of the increased workload and the increased anxiety makes the problems worse. Compound that with any negative self-esteem from yourself not being able to say No, and that's when stress hits.

Stress isn't always obvious. There can be external signs of it, but please realize that only you truly know what is going on in your mind. Prolonged stress can be fatal, either through conditions like heart attacks or through behavioral outcomes such as suicide. It is a problem we should all take seriously.

Stress and low self-esteem can be precursors to depression. Depression is a gray to black zone where you can be an emotional wreck, where sacrifices are useless, and you feel completely hollow from within. Depression needs to be treated by a professional, so do look carefully at the following list of symptoms:

- Over/under-eating
- Always feeling tired
- Loss of interest in otherwise fun or satisfying activities
- Overthinking
- Loss of libido

If you've experienced any of these, it's a good idea to consult a professional for help. You will need all the energy and positivity you can find if you wish to stop sacrificing yourself over and over again, and start living life to the fullest.

Burnout

If you start experiencing some of the things I mentioned above, you will eventually feel like you have just hit the proverbial wall. With nothing going your way, your health being questioned, and the constant fatigue that takes over, you would question yourself whether you are too giving or heading for burnout. Yes, you are heading right there.

It is time to reflect back on things and how they ended up going wrong. So often it can be traced back to your own inability to defend your interest and say No to others.

DRAWING THE LINE

Until and unless you do decide to act, you can never really step out of this zone of self-compromise. Despite all the hardships that you may have faced, despite all that has gone wrong so far, it is never too late to turn things around and get out of this unusual situation.

To change that is always going to be difficult, make no mistake there, but it is never impossible. Being a people pleaser is not bad, but being one around the clock, to almost everyone you get to know, is problematic. It takes away purpose from your own life, and once that happens, you essentially live life to serve others.

Life happens just once, and we don't know when it will come to a stop. If we stop living, stop seeking our purpose, and stop enjoying the delicacies of life, our existence becomes pointless, and that alone is quite a depressing thought. Now it is time to switch the gear and learn something about ourselves. We will dig really deep into ourselves to find out why saying "NO" is so hard.

2

WHY IS IT HARD TO SAY NO?

In the previous chapter, we learned how much we sacrifice when we give in to the demands and requests made by our family members, our friends, and our colleagues. We saw how my dear friend Peter ended up losing a significant sum of money just because he could not find it in himself to say No to his friend.

Life is a matter of balance, and conflict comes when it is imbalanced. We try to balance pleasing others whilst still trying to please ourselves as well. The problem arises when pleasing others overrides our ability to please ourselves: we sacrifice ourselves on the altar of saying Yes.

Saying no can both be intimidating and challenging. It may leave the other person hurt, disappointed, or even angry, and this fear is what normally pushes a person into saying yes, unfortunately, at a cost to their own will and desires.

At the very core of our existence lies simple psychology; we flee from pain and seek out pleasure. We make more effort to ensure we avoid pain than we do in the gaining of pleasure. It's a little weird; it should be the other way around. We may even lie to avoid stress and pain if the situation calls for it, and that leads to a wobbly moral compass that brings its own stress and recriminations.

Pushovers (those who can't say No) are often the first people called to help when something needs to be done. If their self-image is low, the request for help might initially seem like a good thing as they think they are being noticed and appreciated. Then they end up doing a lot of the hard work and rarely get credited or repaid with reciprocated help. This lack of recognition gives the impression they were simply being used, and this has its own jarring impact on their low self-image, which can spiral further downward.

The larger the task they help with, the more time it takes, meaning there is less available time for putting into their own schemes and plans. Saying yes avoids the short-term pain of interpersonal conflict, but it actually creates long-term pain in their own world. The same effort focused on their own goals would reduce stress and help them to climb their own ladder of success.

So let's find out what holds us back from saying no. We will learn about the basic human psychology and how fleeing from pain and being unable to say No fits in. I will also be showing you some of the most common reasons why we actually say yes when we should really have said no instead.

"Knowing is half the battle"

— ANONYMOUS

That's so true. To adequately do something, you first need to learn about it and get to know it. Then our actions count more meaningfully, but we cannot act unless we fully understand what we are dealing with. The next sections will teach us exactly that.

REASONS WHY WE HOLD BACK

To fully understand why we do say yes, even when we dearly wish to say otherwise, we must first know how our minds work. Establishing a good understanding of all that happens within our mind allows us to relate to things a bit easier.

There is a concept that exists which rationally defines how the human mind works when being presented with choices. This concept states that all human beings make decisions either to gain pleasure or to avoid pain and was developed by Sigmund Freud. It is called the Pleasure Principle.

In Freud's psychoanalysis, he suggested that human beings attempt to satisfy their biological and psychological needs. These relate to hunger, thirst, sex, and anger. While all of these basic needs are essential for humans to survive, they are more inclined to make decisions that would help them avoid enduring any pain.

Painkillers are proven to be risky, especially for being used in large amounts and in a long term manner. Still, tremendous amounts of painkillers are being consumed every day worldwide because people need to get rid of pains immediately even though they don't necessarily cure your body. They just help people gain short-term pleasure by numbing their nerves for a while.

The painkiller example is perhaps not your everyday example, but it is to provide you with an idea of just how willing we can be to either gain pleasure or avoid pain. In a similar fashion, when we are at work, or with friends, we do the things we neither like nor prefer, just so we could either avoid the pain of being the odd one out or find pleasure at the end of the act.

At the start, we saw Liam logging Rick into the office system. Despite the fact that Liam did not like the idea of granting him favors, he still went ahead with the action just to avoid letting Rick down. Had he known that the end result of the act would bring in more pain, he may have actually done things differently.

Imagine that when you got a request from either a colleague or a friend, and your answer will really need to be a "No"; what comes into your head? A disappointing look, right? The pain of being guilty follows right away, even though you haven't said anything. To avoid that pain, you immediately switch your "No" into a "Yes" subconsciously and guess what happens: you are saying "Yes" again and again just to avoid the pain of feeling guilty and having to explain and apologize.

When we give in to demands, we normally do not consider how things could be worse. We only hope that things turn out well for us, and completely forget that another possibility looms as well. If we only paid a little more attention, we might just be able to save ourselves a lot of problems. As I said earlier, this is like taking painkillers: it doesn't cure the disease, it just alleviates the pain for a short while. What we really need here is to cure it for good. How we do that is a topic for another chapter, but at least know now that it is quite possible.

When a child is born, the child only seeks out pleasure. The child would need to be fed so that the hunger and thirst subsides. Eventually, the child sleeps to regain their energy. With the passage of time, the child grows up to be an adult, and certainly, other things in life start taking priorities as well. However, with age comes the realization that everyone needs to endure pain in some form. This is where one would either aim to gain pleasure or do anything that may delay or at least diminish the pain, even if that means delayed gratification.

Almost every act we do in our daily lives can be related to this principle, whether it is as simple as brushing our teeth, applying some makeup before heading out for the day, or even going to the gym and working out extensively. All of these are our choices to make, and we do so to gain pleasure, satisfy ourselves, or to avoid pain.

Earlier, I mentioned that we take greater measures to avoid pain than to gain pleasure. I was not making that up either. We go through so much in life that we always fear the mere possibility of pain coming our way. The result is that we would do whatever it takes to avoid unnecessary and immediate pain. Sure, the idea of gaining pleasure may seem motivating, but it is interesting how overshadowed it is by the intensity we feel in acting to avoid foreseeable pain. Slightly surprised? It is a fact!

Jack and you are old-time friends. You have practically grown up together, attended the same schools, college, and even the same university. Both of you are now adults, leading separate lives. While Jack works for a reputable firm, you feel like you can do better by establishing a business for yourself. Being wise, you retain your primary job so that you can support yourself. However, you utilize evenings and weekends to get your start-up going. Every week, you spend your time working hard to lay your start-up on a solid foundation; focus builds that foundation, straying attention does not.

While you're doing two jobs and using your entire waking week, Jack just works Monday to Friday, 9 to 5, then likes to party hard on the weekends. Since you are his best friend, he regularly asks you to join him for nights out on the town. Now going out with Jack won't necessarily harm your side business, but it will definitely delay it.

As the business builds, it grows a little more demanding. Now, more than ever before, you need to commit around eight to ten hours per weekend to ensure you update your website and carry out the necessary tasks, just to keep on top of things. You're in the middle of something and your phone rings: it's Jack with two tickets for a football match. He is on his way to pick you up in an hour. A sudden urge to say No strikes, but you hold yourself back.

"He is my friend, and I can't ruin his mood just because I am too busy!"

With a heavy heart, you say yes, turn your computer off and go dress for the occasion. Effectively, you've just added those necessary hours of today to the necessary hours of tomorrow. This makes matters a little tougher than you may be able to manage. By the time you return home, you're stressing about how to slot in the extra time needed, especially given other commitments you've made for the next few days.

In this case, the fear of losing a friend was nothing but a mere perception. When we make a decision based upon our perception of the pain or pleasure that awaits us, we are constantly reminded that time is of the essence. The closer the situation is to now, the more magnified the feelings tend to be. The business may take quite a while to take off, but your friend was already on the call, leaving you with no time to think — a reason why you were unable to say No.

With time, our perception changes. All of our decisions would always bring either pain or pleasure in more forms than one. These would be short-term pain, long-term pain, short-term pleasure, or long-term pleasure. In the battle of these two stimuli, the short-term tends to be victorious, just as we saw above. The only reason the longer term might win is if you truly understand that the amount of pleasure or pain reduction at the end of the journey is greater.

Both pain and pleasure are triggered emotions. And as we know, emotions trump logic most of the time. In choosing between Jack and the weekend project, we ended up saying yes to Jack because we are more emotionally attached to the friend than we are to the business at that point in time despite logic demanding we focus on the business instead.

WHY DOES THIS HAPPEN?

It's to do with how we are designed. The part of our brain that operates the primitive responses is what our emotions are linked to, and there is no workaround for that. Natural instinct catches up and takes over. The emotions of the here and now override the logic of something that may happen in the future.

If for any reason, our survival is at stake, we would automatically say No to everything else, even if that is Jack or Rick or anyone from home. Our brain shuts down everything else and immediately sends out a signal to respond by fleeing or saving ourselves. You'll know this as the "fight or flight" response. This is the same reason why we eat, drink water, and sleep. When you feel hungry, there is no alternative but to eat. Similarly, if you are thirsty, your body demands water, and we act to satisfy that for the sake of our survival.

Now comes the interesting part, and that is to figure out how all of this helps us to understand why we struggle so much to say No. Throughout this section, we spoke about Freud's Pleasure Principle. We learned how the six various aspects that come into play, all leading us to make decisions based on the given situation at hand.

To remind ourselves what we learned, here is a quick reminder:

- We always try to avoid pain and acquire pleasure.
- Even if we do not gain pleasure, we are always inclined towards avoiding pain.
- Since we have no idea what may cause pleasure or pain, we assume and perceive, and we follow our perception even if flawed.
- After forming a perception, we are further influenced by now rather than the future. Hence we magnify the immediate pleasure or pain.
- If our emotions are involved in the picture, the given element, pleasure or pain, gains intensity without regards to the type or reason.
- In the end, if it comes to the matter of survival, we shut off everything else and focus only on our survival instincts — thanks to the way we are wired with our brains.

This should now make sense the next time you are about to make a decision. If you are asked to cover for someone, and you find yourself struggling to say "No, I can't do that anymore," it is because you are choosing to avoid the pain of being guilty. It is very near to now, and it is your perceived meaning that should you not comply with the request, you would be at the receiving end of harsh and disappointed stares from your co-worker. However, should you find yourself being monitored, even if you wish to help out your friend, you will not. This is where your survival instincts will drive you away, leaving you to worry about the end results later on because you might feel that such an action can get you into a lot of trouble. See how our mind works things out?

This is exactly the reason why we fail to say No in most cases. However, while others may consider this as being humble, nice, and helpful, many consider this as a sign of failure.

"The art of leadership is saying no, not saying yes. It is very easy to say yes."

— TONY BLAIR

In almost every walk of life, saying no is seen as a sign of courage and determination. It is the way where you define your boundaries and lets others know what is acceptable to you and what isn't. It also highlights your core values and allows you to pursue your own purpose in life without being bombarded with additional tasks, unnecessary burdens, and the never-ending and time-consuming favors you may have to grant. With all of that out of the way, you are left with both time and energy to carry on chasing your own success on your own terms.

REASONS WHY WE CAN'T SAY NO

In the previous section, we discovered how easily we make decisions based on certain stimuli, all to help us avoid facing pain, humiliation, or any awkwardness. What about the reasons which compel us to say yes, to give in? What exactly are we trying to avoid or prove by not saying no?

All the big names, Mark Zuckerberg, Steve Jobs, Donald Trump, Winston Churchill, and every name you can come to think of has this one defining ability: to say No without guilt. For us to be successful, it is important to understand that saying no plays a vital role that cannot be achieved or replicated otherwise.

To give you an idea of just how many reasons there are, here are some of the most common ones out there which can genuinely get in the way of you saying no:

1. **Fear of Conflict** - You can either stand your grounds or prepare yourself for conflict. It does not necessarily have to be violent. However, we still fear conflict enough that we flee ourselves away from them. At our core, we just want things to remain normal and friendly, which is why we sacrifice ourselves so that we can avoid a possible conflict.
2. **Fear of Rejection** - This one is more common in professional settings as opposed to more personal ones.

This is where we wish to be in our perceived zone of 'acceptance' and try our very best to ensure we are not rejected by the people around us. Whether it is to cover someone at work, assist someone with their emails, assignments, arguments, or even try to help solve issues that are not concerning to us, we still do it so that we are accepted.

3. **Guilt** - The minute your muster courage to say No, you immediately expose yourself and allow guilt to take over. Now, you will suffer mentally for the rest of the day with guilt for saying no to someone. All of us have been there at least once, if not more. We all try our best to avoid feeling that guilt, which is why we give in to the demands rather easily.

4. **Fear of Losing Opportunities** - Once again, we perceive that we'd be written into the bad books of those who provide employees and society members with opportunities. It is this perception of acquiring a better position in the workplace, home, or society at large, which pushes us to sacrifice ourselves and give in.

5. **Trying to be a Team Player** - When working in a professional setting, you are likely to be a part of a team. This team can either be with you or against you, and that thought alone is enough to convince yourself that you should do as you are told. We go the extra mile and put in extra effort so that we can be

considered as a team player. Good intentions, but they hurt us in the long run.

6. **Genuine Intention to Help** - Yet again, we take our good intentions to help and go on saying yes to others, without considering that we may be encouraging someone else to be more laid back or do something less productive. We may also be encouraging others around us to let them burden us while they sit back and relax. In the end, we are the only people who suffer from it.

7. **Respecting Others** - Out of sheer respect for others, we often feel like we have no choice but to give in to their demands or requests. How often do you find yourself doing that? I imagine quite a lot.

8. **Trying to Prove Your Worthiness** - People who join new offices or who have just been promoted find themselves full of motivation. This motivation is often misinterpreted by such people, which is why they go on working more than they need to so that they can prove they belong there. This would then include covering for their co-workers, filling out reports for someone else, handling extra tasks on their own, and all that while doing their own work as well. Surely, something has to give at some point? Yes, probably you.

9. **Just Not Willing to Say No** - I have observed that people from different cultures or backgrounds often

find it impossible to say No. To them, doing so goes against their moral and ethical values. True, there is no reason to go against such values, but helping someone do something that can be done once. If the same person approaches you over and over, it is clear that they now rely on you to do their work for them. That is where things need to stop. However, people still continue to help just because they have to.

10. **It Is Just Hard** - It may be hard for you, and it most certainly would be harder for women, but this is where we need to remind ourselves that this is nothing more than a perceived concept. Men and women find it hard to say No to others, especially to the opposite gender. We are always trying to be nice and helpful, which once again leads us to struggle when met with a request. We just smile while our heart sinks, and we give in as we reassure that we will have the task handled.

Whatever the reason may be, saying no apparently seems to be tougher than one might think. With that said, it is certainly not impossible. All it needs is a bit of practice, a bit of will and a hint of dedication, and before you know, you would be saying no with confidence.

IN SUMMARY

Before we started this chapter, a lot of us may never have come across the Pleasure Principle. After having gone through how our mind works and how we prefer choosing pain avoidance over acquiring pleasure, it makes a lot more sense why we ultimately say yes as opposed to no. We develop this irrational fear within ourselves, which holds us back from saying what we really want to say. If anything, we are trying to flee from saying no. Moving forward, we will no longer be doing that. We will be taking a head-on approach and deal with matters the way they should be.

So far, you have been able to see just how much damage you can suffer just for not being able to say No. You feel guilty, you feel awkward, but those who continuously ask you for those petty favors, they don't feel any of that. It is time to step up, regain control of your life, and start living once again.

You have everything you need to get started. I know, the fact that you are going through this book proves that you have the will and the desire to lead a better life. You have taken out enough time to find out the answers, and that is exactly what I intend to provide in the coming chapters. I only wanted to provide you with enough reasons and facts to know just how much you have been losing without actually realizing any of it.

Now you know, it is time to act. In the next chapter, we will begin our first step towards learning how to say No confidently.

We will discover just how life can change and the fringe benefits you can expect to come your way. We will explore how you can truly learn about what you value more and what matters to you. Knowing that would allow you to pursue exactly the kind of life you wish to live and have all the confidence in the world. Let us get ready to start preparing our minds and fine-tune our way of thinking to become assertive.

3

MENTAL PREPARATION FOR SAYING NO

We've learned why it is so hard to say no, and we now understand that we avoid pain more than we seek pleasure. We're in a position, at last, to take practical steps towards meaningful change. At the heart of every decision is choice, and choices come from our mindset and belief system. In order to change from saying yes to saying no, we need to change our mindset and belief system first. So let's take some time to prepare our mindset and become mentally equipped for that.

The first step takes courage, determination, and the will to execute. Once you take that first step, the next steps get easier. You don't know your potential yet and how you can change the course of your life. This chapter will provide you with all the information needed to prepare yourself to say no with some exercises to collect your thoughts, re-discover your personal goals, values, and get reconnected to your own true self. By the end of the chapter, you will feel better about yourself, gaining the confidence you need to take the next step with finesse and style. You'll be turning heads when people see the new you.

PATH TO REDISCOVERY

The approach detailed below is the process I went through with the groups of people I trained. They too answered the same questions I'm posing you here, and after they were done answering, they kept this information until the very end of the training. At that point, we reviewed the answers from people who wished to share them, which most of the group did. In every group, we learned some interesting new facts about one another, often realizing just how disconnected we were from our own core values and goals. After the training sessions, it was amazing to see how much confidence the group had to start doing exactly what they had always wanted to do.

Some members switched their careers. Some ended bad relationships and went on to find more suitable partners. Some started new hobbies while others enrolled themselves in fitness classes. The results were astonishing. You, too, will realize how much you have missed out on and what led you to make such choices in the first place. Let's dive in a little deeper.

We're going to do an exercise, after which you will feel alive and empowered. We'll wipe the slate clean, emptying our minds of all the thoughts and memories which have held it back. A busy mind will struggle to absorb new ideas and concepts, so we're going to calm it and give it the chance it needs.

> *"Empty your cup so that it may be filled; become devoid to gain totality"*
>
> — BRUCE LEE

Find a quiet place to sit away from distractions. Use dim lighting if that promotes peace; natural light flowing in through the windows also works well. Ensure you have a pen and a notebook or a piece of paper for any thoughts that may come.

Sit comfortably, and consciously relax your muscles. Close your eyes. Breathe in and out slowly and deeply with the time for inhalation roughly equal to the time for exhalation. That means if breathing in takes about four seconds, then breathe out for four seconds as well. It does not have to be precisely four seconds: you choose the timings that lets you breathe in and out slowly and comfortably.

With each breath in, think of something that is weighing on your mind, and with each breath out, let that thought go. Breathe in – think of the problem; breathe out – release the problem. Continue this for about two minutes, ensuring your eyes remain closed.

Feels better, doesn't it? If this is the first time you're trying this type of exercise, you may not be totally calm and empty, but almost everyone will be calmer and emptier. And you can always get better with practice. When you're in the calmer state, let yourself know that everything has a reset button; that when you press the reset button, you have the ability to unwind those thoughts and feelings that have held you back. You can shape the new you: a more assertive, knowledgeable, and confident person.

We'll shape this persona with your own thoughts and desires. "Persona" can sound a little intimidating, but it really isn't – it just means being who you are with the good qualities emphasized and the poor qualities reduced or rejected. We'll also give this persona any qualities we lacked initially.

You're now ready to explore yourself, so let's start with some basic questions. Time is less important than honesty, so take all the time you need to answer them as honestly as you can. Remember, it is you we are talking about, and no-one knows you better than yourself. Your answers will soon start showing you things you may not have noticed before. Write these answers down – later on, you may wish to reflect on where you started from and how things have changed for you. Here are the questions to get you started:

1. Are you always worried about what people may think about you?
2. Are you always trying to please people to make them feel good about you?
3. Do you base your choices in relationships, careers, and otherworldly activities on pleasing others or impressing them?
4. If all the worries in the world were to vanish, what would you like to do?
5. What do you really like about yourself?
6. Would you pursue or even enjoy pursuing a career of your choice?
7. What career would that be?
8. If you were not being judged, what would you love to do today?

Don't move on until you've worked through those questions. You might not get through them all in one session – that's totally fine. Come back to it tomorrow and continue where you left off. When you're ready, it's time to change your perspective.

. . .

Perspective

Perspective is the ability to see things in a new light, from a new standpoint. It helps us to see things for what they really are. Often, a change in perspective is all that's needed to start the change in ourselves as we realize the error of the previous belief.

Take, for instance, your perspective of your self-image in others' eyes. If you're a people pleaser, you might think that your "Yes" to them is putting you in their good books and building relationships between you and them. That, however, is unlikely: their perspective of you is far different from that. Instead of going into their good books, you're actually in their "take advantage" book. Instead of building relationships with them, you are ruining your relationships with them by lowering your value in their eyes. Ask yourself the questions: do they care you as much as you do about them? Do they care what you think as much as you do about their thoughts? The answer will most likely be a NO. Realize this, see the new perspective, and suddenly it's much easier to match our efforts to their efforts as we care about them to the same degree they care about us – which isn't a lot!

Now, this will blow your mind a bit: as you care less and withdraw, you'll find a strange thing happen. They actually start to care *more*; they start to respect you more and see you from a different perspective than they did previously. Their mindset is also changed and becomes much more in line with your own.

There is a greater balance between you and them, and therefore greater potential for a real relationship. With this new balance and new potential, you will be very fascinated by the new depth and quality of the relationship that grows between you.

A simple change was all we needed. By keeping things in perspective, we allow ourselves to feel less burdened about trying to make others think better about us. Grab your notebook and write down any insights you have on perspective. To help you dig deeper, please try to answer the following questions.

- Am I too obsessed with pleasing my friends and family members?
- An especially important question to be honest about with yourself.
- Have I set limits and boundaries for others?
- We all have set some limits, but think deeper. Do these boundaries need to be explained to the other person clearly and vocally?
- Have I been honest with the people that matter about my inner feelings?
- Do you go along with other people's choices to not make them feel bad? Would it have been better to speak up and give your honest thoughts and feelings, but you didn't? If so, note it down: this is a key point to rebalancing unbalanced relationships.

- How has my perspective changed after answering all the previous questions?
- Which relationships will this new perspective have an impact on?

Find Your Values

Everyone has certain rules and core values which define the kind of person they are now and who they become later. These are values that we continuously follow and abide by, and the most successful of us know and follow their values best. Values can change, but they are slow to change as they are ingrained within us. Clearly, to remain true to your values, you must discover what they are.

Even after our values are discovered, we may lose sight of them and do things we would never have done otherwise. This can have an impact on our relationships: for instance, repeated lying may mean people start losing their trust and respect for this person and withdraw their friendship. If one would remain true to their values, such things would never manifest.

If you have strayed too far from your values, you can take action to return to them. It might take effort, but it's worth it. You may even go so far as to set new values if you see gaps in your moral armory. Here are some questions to help you think in this regard.

- What makes me feel motivated?

- Discover what you know and identify as your true sources of motivation, be it friends, your partner, a hobby, a long-lost passion. Anything that interests you or gets you fired up.
- What brings out the best in me?
- Is this involvement in your social circle, a specific task you do, or a character trait such as seeing and wanting to help people in need. Prioritize your list.

Your Goals Matter

Whatever goals we've set for ourselves with time, we may have lost sense of what they were and taken a different path altogether. We continue to do things to please others, to gain favor or more favorable opinions of ourselves from others, all the while forgetting that our goals matter just as much as others, maybe even more.

What you must understand is that your goals will not be catered to by anyone else. You will need to take the time out and put in the energy to achieve these goals, and only you will feel the excitement and that sense of accomplishment. Others would only be there to applaud while having no idea what achieving such goals might mean to you.

Suppose you are a working mom. You are already devoted to your children, and you have a good career going on that operates from home. Don't do favors for others just because you know them. You need a substantial reason that makes sense and provides you a sense of achievement after completing that task for your friend or associate. If it is something you like to do and worth your time, it is okay to proceed; but just because you wish to please a friend or help out someone in need is not enough of a reason. Your own goals remain and should matter the most to you, period.

Sure, it can be quite hard to place your goals above everything else at first. You might even feel a bit selfish, but that is perfectly okay. *Allow yourself to feel the need and necessity of your goals.* Let your goals stand out from the rest and allow yourself to completely focus on them without letting anyone else interrupt you. Only then would you truly be able to learn how to avoid those excessive burdening tasks because you would know just how important your own goals are and how much they mean to you. Answering the following questions will help you think more comprehensively.

- Do I know my goals?
- We are not talking here about possible promotions or buying a house. These are universal goals and apply to everyone. Think a little wider. Seek out goals that truly motivate you to do go the extra mile and give you purpose. These goals should not be short-lived.
- What do I wish to achieve in the next year?
- This answer would vary from person to person, but try and remain as realistic as possible.
- What do I wish to achieve in the next five years?

- What are the top three qualities about myself that need greater exploration?
- By learning about these qualities, you will have somewhere to start from. You can then go on to build upon these skills or qualities accordingly.

Never compare your capabilities to others. You are unique in your own right. Just because someone can do something better does not mean that you can produce the same results. You may just be exceptionally good at something else; all you need is the time to figure your skills and your goals out.

Your Priorities Take Priority

By now, if you have been following the previous chapters closely, you would already know what your priorities are and that you should focus more on your priorities than others'. When someone approaches you, you're immediately ready to convey that you already have enough on your plate.

"I am sorry, but that would be a no. My to-do list is overflowing, and I can't take on any additional tasks at the moment. I might be able to fit something in in a few days, but I'm swamped right now."

When a person knows these priorities, they can say no with conviction. By doing so, this person would know that his/her own priorities are more beneficial and worth the attention. However, to ensure this works all the time, you must know your goals and such priorities clearly. And then, like a lawyer doing a pro bono case, if you decide to indulge the requestor with a Yes instead, it's controlled by you and is implemented under your terms and conditions.

To set these priorities right, you can pay attention to how these priorities will impact you and those around you. You can gauge how much it would mean to you and those near you if you fulfill these tasks. If it helps, write these down in your to-do list and rank these according to their significance.

By maintaining a to-do list, or even a calendar, you would know that you already have important matters to cater to, and then you will always be able to say No without feeling guilty.

Confidence, Honesty, And Perseverance

Confidence allows you to channel your inner self and do things with authority and command. It all comes down to the value that you place on yourself. The higher that value, the higher your confidence.

> *"I say if I'm beautiful. I say if I'm strong. You will not determine my story - I will."*
>
> — AMY SCHUMER

Now, this is interesting. Anyone can gain the confidence to speak publicly, to express their views to others, AND to say no without feeling guilty or sorry for the other party.

Confidence is best founded on a platform of honesty. Lies and deception undermine your ability to become and to remain confident – even the threat of being found to be lying is enough to shake your confidence. The simplest way is to remain as honest as possible, though this is not always the easiest path to follow.

Confidence and honesty provide a solid platform to stand on. Perseverance is needed to reach the goals we set for ourselves. All the content and practices in this book can help you build confidence for your first couple of times to convert your previous yes to a no. But as time goes by, you may come to a point when your confidence is not as high. This is when perseverance kicks in by not letting the changes that we've worked so hard to make thus far, fall by the wayside. We need to push through the desire for immediate gratification and strengthen our wills to continue defying the odds and proving our worth and capabilities.

IN SUMMARY

We've learned on the path to rediscovery that creating a persona that is ready to take on challenges and is set to face the world with confidence and assertiveness relies on five core values. These successful personas remain honest to themselves first and foremost. They are always motivated and highly enthusiastic enough that people around them can sense it themselves. They are known to work hard and intelligently and focus on result-oriented tasks instead of wasting time on things that don't align with their values. They are people confident in making decisions quickly and without regret or guilt. They persevere for years if they have to, but in the end, they acquire the success they had targeted.

LETTING GO OF PERFECTION

As Abraham Lincoln said in quoting the poet John Lydgate

> *"You can please some of the people all of the time,*
>
> *you can please all of the people some of the time,*
>
> *but you can't please all the people all of the time"*

No one is perfect – we all have errors, flaws, and tendencies to make mistakes. So here's one of the ironies of people-pleasing: by pleasing some people, almost by definition, you are displeasing other people. So how can you be perfect and please everyone? The simple truth is, you can't.

Initially, when I posed this question at a seminar, it stunned a few members of the audience when they realized perfection is nothing more than an illusion. Even when you give your 100% to serve others, someone will always judge you, and someone will be frowning or even enraged by what you have done. That is life. So who are you really pleasing?

Knowing that someone will always take offense at what you've done or will disagree with, it may be the wake-up call you need to stop caring so much about what other people think. Hopefully, you'll now realize that even as you try your hardest, it isn't good enough for someone. Furthermore, you won't always be able to try your hardest: you're not superwoman or superman. If pleasing everyone is the goal, we're bound to fail.

Give this message time to soak in. After all, you have spent most of your life living on a principle of pleasing others and sacrificing yourself. It will be quite a change. The outcome of that change means you can start to prioritize what matters to you and the tasks you want to get done in life. Once you start working on what's important to you, you will gain greater confidence to say no to others' workloads, chores, or tasks, meaning you're more likely to meet your own set targets for the day.

Remember as well, each one of us is designed with a unique set of strengths and weaknesses, so if you're asked to do something by someone, it might be that they're pretty good at the task and think it won't take you long because it wouldn't take them long.

In that case particularly, it makes more sense for the person asking to do the work themselves.

Saying No Isn't Necessarily Selfish

If you think focusing on yourself is selfish, please stop now. If you never think of others at all, then that accusation may hold some water. This is not what we're talking about here – we're talking about healthy self-centeredness where polite assertiveness for the things that matter to you is a good thing.

If you were to decline an invitation to a party with friends, would you wonder if those friends would ever invite you again? If something important is keeping you from their party, then use your honesty to let them know that – they'll appreciate the gesture, and although you miss the party, you may well have strengthened your friendship. Then again, if you're turning down the party because you actually don't want to be there, then does it matter whether they invite you again?

Here is a simple rule for everyone to note down and remember: the less there is on your plate, the less the stress you have. By saying no, not only are you focusing on your own tasks and important matters at home, in society, or at work, but you are also allowing yourself to reduce your stress. This isn't selfish – it's sensible!

WHAT'S THE WORST THAT COULD HAPPEN

You've confronted your inner demons and reordered your internal world to gain confidence and are now ready to say no for the first time. If initially there's the fear of what could happen when you finally say the magical word, then let's break things down and see just how bad things could turn out to be. You might be pleasantly surprised to know that things will not be as bad as you thought.

Negative comments are probably the reaction you'll get the most. But instead of worrying about them, or paying attention to them, look at things in a factual way. The comments others pass reflect their world view, not yours. If they're making harsh comments, it's probably more a reflection of bad experiences in their own life. That is to say that their world view may not necessarily be the brightest.

You can take a negative comment. You've dug down deep during this process and have probably been a far harsher critic of yourself than the others are being now. In fact, you will be pleasantly surprised by how ineffective their negative comments are. If that's the worst they can do, it's not that bad.

Loss of a friendship could be one of the outcomes. In truth, there isn't much to say other than if saying no loses you a friend, then they weren't much of a friend to begin with, and you're far better off without their friendship. In my circle of friends, the freedom to say no is critical to our continued friendship. We wouldn't dream of dumping a friendship for this reason. Quite the contrary, it earns our respect and forbearance.

Life, A Limited Stay

You only get one shot at this life. There are no rewind buttons nor retry buttons. Live life to the fullest and pass by the naysayers. Unless what they say is productive, it serves no purpose at all, so treat it as background noise from a busy road: you hear the traffic, but you also don't really hear it.

Get up, gather the courage, and seek out your passion. Say no to anything getting in your way.

IN SUMMARY

This chapter focused on how our minds perceive things and how we can train it to take a leap of faith and create a completely new mindset. Remember, if you can think straight and true, there is nothing that can stand in your way. So prepare your mind to veto requests – then you'll know when the time comes, and you'll be able to express that externally as "No", without lies, just 100% honesty. Savor the moment once you do because the first time is always exhilarating.

Saying no allows you to value and honor your existing or current obligations. These could be related to your family time, a dinner at a friend's place, a social gathering, or anything else. Reserved time for matters important to you and say no to continue honoring your commitments, ensuring nothing gets in the way unless it is a dire emergency.

Your path to rediscovery can both be fascinating and intimidating. The prospect of waking up to a completely new life may sound alarm bells and keep you up through the night. Let me be the first to tell you that you do not need to fear anything. The worst is already in the past; what awaits you next is beyond exceptional.

In the next chapter, we will start looking into the power of boundaries and how we can set them with a simple no as a response.

4

SET YOUR BOUNDARIES, WHEN TO SAY NO

"Good fences make good neighbors."

— "MENDING WALL"- ROBERT FROST

One of the most common issues I have observed personally with people who struggle to say no is that most of them are actually struggling in another area: setting boundaries. Most of them have no idea what boundaries are, where they are applicable, and how one can set boundaries or limits, up without offending others. This is what we'll be learning in this chapter and how boundaries can help us lead a better life individually, financially, personally, and professionally. There will be an exercise at the end of the chapter, which will let you reflect on all that you have learned. Think about how you can use the acquired information to find out your own boundaries, so be sure to keep that pen and notebook handy.

When it comes to boundaries, we all set them differently: I may find something acceptable, which you do not. Similarly, women may set different boundaries for men and vice versa. Limits can be emotional; they can be physical, even spiritual. Ultimately you decide how firm or lenient they are. Imagine these boundaries as a filter that only lets through particular aspects of life while blocking the others from ever entering your mind.

When setting boundaries, recognize what you can change and what you cannot will help you make peace with the unchangeable and increase your determination to change what can be to make a difference. There are different cultural norms where some societies observe one practice, and other cultures observe other practices, especially in the manner in which men interact with women. For example, some cultures don't mind if men shake hands with or hug women, and other cultures prefer a more conservative recognition of physical boundaries. Cultural and societal boundaries are not something we generally have much control over.

How we were brought up is often a key determinant in how effective we are at setting limits for others. In the early part of our lives, we don't have much control over boundary setting for ourselves – instead, the people in authority around us set the limits: our own parents or guardians, parents of our friends and neighbors, teachers, and other leaders such as those in Scouts or Girl Guides. As we grow into our teens, and further as we move upwards into college and finally into the workplace, how boundaries are set and who set them changes. In our personal lives, we do. We engage in activities that allow us to be ourselves. Whether it is socializing with a specific group of people, or choosing to pursue a degree, even the relationships we want, all of these are choices we make. We make them based on our own moral and ethical values. Boundaries in our relationship with a partner are particularly important: setting them too loose will likely result in being taken advantage of, but setting them too strict will repel our partner. Neither is good in the extreme. However, the good news is, with some thought and a bit of effort, balanced boundaries can be established, which will strengthen our relationships.

It is interesting to note how our boundary setting inherently says something about ourselves. Keep rigid and strict boundaries, adopt a zero-tolerance approach, and you portray yourself someone deeply insecure. The other extreme is not received positively either. So let's take a look at how we can set healthy boundaries.

Setting Healthy Boundaries

Healthy boundaries are the kind of boundaries that provide you with balance, giving you and others a chance to interact with respect. By setting up healthier boundaries, not only are you letting everyone know more about you as a person, but you are also encouraging others to maintain mutual respect and ethical awareness. Just as a physical boundary fence reduces the risk of unwanted people wandering into your property, your physical space, so do social boundaries for your mental space. During the global COVID-19 pandemic, it was never easier to understand how physical boundaries can be healthy, so healthy that they're life-saving. Social distancing was quite literally keeping your health and life by setting a physical boundary.

Developing healthy boundaries improves mental and emotional stability, which should be your first two primary objectives. Strong boundaries portray a more dynamic and positive image of you to others. These also help establish your identity and individuality. Such boundaries allow you to clearly convey to others what you can be held responsible for and what lies beyond your control.

Other benefits accrued from effective boundary setting include:

- Communicating your needs with the partner in your relationship
- Allowing one to practice self-care and respect
- Allowing time management for positive interactions
- Clarifying doubts

- Discouraging acts like sexual advancements or harassment
- Maintaining your own privacy
- Improving self-esteem and confidence
- Becoming assertive
- Empowering you to make better choices
- Empowering you to say no to poor choices

Draw a clear line of what you can accept, and what you find completely unacceptable, and most people would honor those limitations. Interestingly, this may remove your need to say no: if people know where your boundaries are, and they know a particular request will take them over that boundary, then most likely, they won't even ask the question since they already know the answer.

I tend to be a very calm and patient person, but if I come across an act of bullying or racism, I know it is unacceptable and in violation of my boundaries. So I speak up, refusing to remain quiet, and letting the other party know immediately that they have crossed the line. Most sensible people would retreat and apologize, but even for those who may not do so, they will promptly know what is acceptable to me and what is not.

So how do you set these boundaries? While we will discuss different scenarios in the next section, it is important to first understand how things work and how you can define your boundaries to others.

Boundaries are implemented in the following manner:

1. Define your boundaries by identifying them yourself first. There's an exercise at the end of the chapter which should help you to reflect and decide upon your own boundaries. Use the answers to see a pattern and pick out things that matter to you the most.
2. Where appropriate, communicate the boundary information to the relevant people. Say to them what you're ok with, and what you're not ok with, in a calm and simple way. There is no need to over-explain things.
3. If necessary, explain to them the outcome of what crossing the line will do to your relationship. This will help to emphasize why these boundaries are important.

THE NECESSARY BOUNDARIES

Boundaries are necessary between us and those we interact with in a meaningful way: our sphere of influence. We interact with them at differing depths and with differing importance. Let's take a look at some of them.

Boundaries With Colleagues

We spend so long in our workplace, more than a third of each week, that establishing good boundaries here is important. Setting healthy limits here reduces the likelihood of being bullied by others or being a target of criticism and cruel remarks. Healthy boundaries promote productivity and ensure a stress-free ambiance for all. It is quite likely that your employer will have a Code of Conduct which lays out the expectation of management how staff will interact and behave. This guiding document forms the basis of workplace behaviors, although it is not possible to completely legislate for every interaction. There is generally an expectation that people will treat each other with respect and dignity, and in so doing, be able to decide and develop all the other norms that guide office behavior. Some good examples of the latter include:

- No work over the weekends
- No work-related banter outside work, especially when with family

- Saying no to opportunities which clearly do not suit your way of living
- Properly utilizing paid leaves
- Close the door for a bit of silence when you really need it
- Sticking to your own perception of balancing both work and personal life
- No physical contact rule

The work-related boundaries are divided into three categories. These are:

Job Responsibilities - The type of boundaries which either managers or individuals set for themselves and those around them. Managers could create boundaries for those reporting to them, and these may include things like:

- Whom do you report to?
- Who is to assign the work for the day?
- Who gives you the feedback?
- Who makes the decisions regarding what tasks you should be working on?

Once these are in place, employees can further create their own boundaries to work effectively and efficiently. These boundaries could include:

- Informing others not to contact you after work hours

- Refusing projects or additional tasks if you already have a lot on your plate
- Approaching your immediate manager regarding possible violations

Interpersonal Boundaries - These are the kind of boundaries that we set between ourselves and our co-workers. These are also the types of boundaries that are healthy to have between employees and managers. Such boundaries revolve around factors such as:

- Using a specific tone of voice within your workplace
- The type of attitude people should have towards each other
- To continue performing duties with members of your office with whom you may have personal differences
- Limiting your conversations during work to work-related topics

Personal Boundaries - These are exclusively your own boundaries, which allow you to maintain a healthy balance between work and life itself. These can include things such as:

- Ensuring you leave your work laptop/computer at work
- Planning and taking vacations to actually be away from work

- Limiting your social media and email access
- Limiting your access to work-related emails or chats when not working

Boundaries With Subordinates

When you find yourself in a competitive environment, you are bound to come across people who would seek your approval or assistance to gain some advantage over others. Try not to promote such behavior and remain neutral and honest. For everyone's best interest, let them know that you cannot assist because if you do, it would be downright unfair to those who are working hard to perform their part of the duties with honesty.

You can expect such situations more commonly if you are:

- A mentor
- A manager
- Playing a role of authority

Boundaries With Clients

If your work revolves around handling various clients, either for your own business or for an organization that you work for, you will need to set up certain boundaries to ensure you maintain your professional composure and don't do anything that may cause issues later on.

To set such boundaries, reflect on a few questions:

- What are your working hours?
- When is it feasible for you to be approached by your clients?
- How should a client contact you?
- Would you be okay with answering your client's calls after working hours?
- Would you accept urgent requests?

Reflecting on these questions would allow you to get a clearer picture of what is acceptable to you and what isn't. Depending on your answers, you can set these boundaries and communicate the same through emails or phone calls. Your client should have no issues following these.

There are cases where people step out of their own boundaries and try to go the extra mile. Most of them end up with clients who continue to ask for urgent work, and they continue to push the boundaries. Eventually, such a person becomes frustrated and overburdened. The end result can spell out disaster in terms of business. In this circumstance approaching a manager to explain the problems with workload can mean that steps are taken to improve how the business interacts with clients. Ultimately this decision is set at a company level and can then be explained to a demanding client.

These boundaries need to be established and communicated right at the start of your correspondence with the potential client. These boundaries then need to be maintained even if you are dealing with your regular clients. Allowing yourself or your client to break a boundary would mean that you are inviting the other party to continue violating these boundaries.

When communicating what your boundaries are, be as clear as possible. If there is a corporate document outlining what's required of you that you can send to the client, then send it: it will explain much on your behalf. Do not provide vague explanations to your clients. Try and be as effective as a communicator as you can. These will help ensure that your client knows what they can expect from you.

Remember, you may be paid significantly, but that is never enough to be someone's personal assistant around the clock. By communicating your boundaries at the start, you will allow yourself to lead a stress-free post-work life, knowing that you will not be bothered by anyone.

Boundaries With Spouse

When coming to the boundaries with our spouse, most of us are worried that those boundaries may create estrangement between our partners and us, which leads to weakening our connection. As we mentioned quite a lot of times in this book, healthy boundaries will strengthen our bond, and boost our relationship with our partner. These boundaries may include:

- The topics and behaviors when in public
- For example, you might want to avoid talking about your private issues while you are outside with other people, such as bills left to pay, chores needed to be done, etc. You may also want to avoid behaviors that have sexual suggestiveness in public. This may differ for people.
- How you communicate
- This is very important since the wrong ways of communication will harm people's feelings and even the quality of relationships. A good example is you and your partner may want to avoid increasing your voice regardless of how angry you are.
- Responsibilities at home
- A balanced and fair relationship is healthier than those in which one feels being taken advantage of. A simple example will be if somebody does the cooking, then the other one needs to wash the dishes.

There is still a lot more that you can expand on this, such as the boundary of sexual intimacy, personal time, support of relatives.

Boundaries With Friends

Yes, even with your dearest friends, there are certain boundaries that are to be kept, communicated, and maintained to have a healthy, friendly relation continue. Quite a few tend to have virtually no boundaries or have completely weak ones in place.

Such friendships do not last long and can often lead to chaotic results.

Just like most relations, one must always set out physical and emotional boundaries when it comes to friends. These boundaries not only allow a person to feel better, but they also let others feel happier and more comfortable. Most boundaries, when it comes to friends, are set naturally. You do not really need to put in much effort, but when it comes to defining physical boundaries, you will need to come up with ways to communicate those clearly.

These boundaries can include:

- Avoiding any physically abusive acts or behavior
- Avoiding verbal abuse
- No gossiping behind each other's back
- Being honest without being blunt to avoid hurting feelings

These are quite universal in nature, and almost every friend would have such boundaries in place for each other. However, enforcing these is where people often go wrong.

It is okay to remind each other what these boundaries are once in a while. If you feel like your friends are pushing you and your boundaries, remind them that such behavior will only cause issues and that you are not going to let your boundaries down just because you are friends with them. You can let them know that you respect their boundaries and would prefer the same to be reciprocated.

Use a subtle tone to remind your friends when they cross a line. Do not go out shouting or screaming at them as that will effectively ruin your friendship. A great social circle is one that promotes the best in you, not the opposite. If you feel like you are the best version of yourself when you are with your friends, you have chosen well. If you find that you are anything but the best version of your inner self, it might be time to start thinking of cutting such people off or at least putting some distance between you and them.

Successful people choose to remain with others who only provide genuine advice and bring the best out of a person. This is why you would never see big CEOs and directors letting their guard down regardless of the scenario.

If you have accidentally set rigid boundaries, there is always room for compromise. However, know that you will only need to compromise on your rigid boundaries to restore balance and not to let others take advantage of you or use you for their gains.

Boundaries With Neighbors

Having great neighbors is a blessing. You know you can always have someone you can trust when the time comes, and you need assistance. You may not have realized this, but you may just be a good neighbor yourself for someone near you. They also may be trusting you to remain honest and friendly. However, even here, there are certain boundaries that we need to create. Remember, the point of having boundaries is to ensure that no one crosses the line and that you have all the confidence and right should the situation call for you to say no.

Boundaries with neighbors can include things such as:

- Borrowing policy - Setting rules on whether you would be borrowing items from your neighbors. If so, you would need to ensure you return the items in their original condition. You will need to reciprocate here, and that is where your boundaries will help you ensure they follow the same rules as well.
- Receiving mail on your behalf - It is only natural that you cannot be expected to remain home all the time. There may be an important delivery that is made when you are not around. If you believe your neighbor is honest, you can set boundaries and let them know that they can collect packages or mail when you are not home. You can do the same for them should they ever leave the house, and something important comes along. What you will need to enforce is that such packages and mail remain untouched and unopened. Unless instructed otherwise, you should not take a peek inside. If you do this, your neighbors would probably do the same to you.
- Noise limits - You have rights just as your neighbors

do. Let them know that you are okay with a certain amount of noise and that if they are to host a party that may end late, you should be notified beforehand to avoid inconvenience.
- Privacy - You may be someone who values your privacy, but you may have a neighbor who continuously keeps an eye on things happening around your house. You can convey your concerns and let them know that they would appreciate a watchful eye as long as it is not invading anyone's privacy.

There can be many other boundaries that you can set between yourself and your neighbors. By maintaining such boundaries, you will lead a more relaxed lifestyle at home, without worrying about what may be going on in your neighborhood or if someone is trying to take a peek inside your house.

IN SUMMARY

Boundaries, physical, emotional, or psychological in nature, allow you to lead a life on your own terms. You get to choose what is appropriate and what is not. Those around you will follow and respect these boundaries in the main. Yes, there can be pushback, but as long as you maintain your boundaries and draw your lines in the sand, you should face no issues in resolving these petty problems.

If you remember, in the beginning, I mentioned that we would be going through an exercise at the end of this chapter. We learned all about boundaries and how they help us out. Now, it is time for you to grab your pen and paper and start finding your own boundaries.

Create a table where one side consists of the boundaries you would like to set for various people/scenarios such as work, neighbors, friends, family, etc. On the other side of the table, note down aspects which are important to you, that you are comfortable working with and in line with your core values. You can refer to the examples above to get more inspiration.

This table will serve you as a reminder of what you truly feel is acceptable and thus allowing you to establish such boundaries and communicate the same to the people concerned.

So far, you have worked on building a solid foundation. You are now ready to start learning about how you can say no effectively and without ever feeling guilty about any part of it. In the next chapter, we will go through some of the most useful strategies which allow almost anyone to gain the confidence and the willpower to stand their ground and say no without offending anyone. We will not be resorting to lies. Instead, we will be looking into clever strategies that convey the message clearly and still make it sound acceptable to anyone.

We are not here to make 'something' out of life. We are here to make 'everything' out of life — the way we had always dreamed.

These boundaries play a pivotal role in our lives as they help us establish our identity as an individual. They also reflect our mental health and well-being, which is why having the right type of boundaries would always push us forward, to live as opposed to existing.

5

THE STRATEGIES OF SAYING NO, WHAT TO SAY

Finally, the time has come where we start learning ways to say no, the reason behind our journey here in the first place. If you have gone through all the previous chapters, you should have a good idea of how you need to prepare yourself and communicate your thoughts. However, if you decided to jump to this chapter directly, I would recommend that you go back to the previous chapters first. It is likely that we will be coming across a few terms or concepts which would make no sense unless you learn about them first.

This chapter will finally pit us against our fears and teach us how to dominate the challenging situation of saying no. It will also talk about various strategies of saying no without offending anyone. *There are many ways to say no. You just need to focus on identifying the right strategy for the right time.* We will be using all that we have already learned, such as setting boundaries and acquiring the right mindset to ensure that we are able to say no confidently, without any second thoughts, with a smile on our faces and a winning attitude.

THE BEST WAYS TO SAY NO

Each situation you face comes with unique characteristics. Every time you receive a request, a favor, or a potential overload of work, you are left with almost no time to think matters through or plan a response. Most often, it's this lack of time that pushes us to agree to the request instead of saying no. We stumble around looking for an excuse, don't find one, and then capitulate; instead, we should have prepared, honest responses available for these situations.

You are putting your heart and soul into changing your life. Prepare answers in advance and maintain your high degree of integrity with open, honest responses. This will help you make decisions easily and, when needed, say no to others.

Saying "I don't" As Opposed To "I can't"

Both of these mean two different things and portray two completely separate images. Both are fine, although when you use them depends on the situation. With "I don't", you are saying no to something because it either goes against your own values. On the other hand, you have a word that describes your inability to carry out the task.

The word "don't" usually serves you better in the long run. Whatever the situation may be, by saying that you don't do something allows you to reiterate your own priorities, values, and goals which you intend to pursue instead. It also helps you in setting healthy boundaries as opposed to saying no directly because now the person asking will know in the future that that type of request is off-limits for you.

Add Some Compliments

When was the last time you asked someone to help you out with something but ended up receiving an answer you never expected?

"Jill, you don't need my help at all. This is a fairly simple task, and I am sure you will do it nicely."

Isty, a friend of mine, was an absolute genius at this approach, and it was hysterical listening to him turning people down. By the time he'd finished letting them down gently, they were convinced that not only was it better that they had been let down, but were excited by the opportunity to do the task they had originally had in mind for Isty. He was brilliant. Now we can't all be that good, but Isty's approach was based on solid reasoning – all people have their own skillset and responsibilities and with some thought and application, most are able to come up with a plan to get the task done on time and to the required standard. And that approach is complimentary and empowering – it leaves us motivated that we can do it on our own.

Always be polite when saying no; speak your mind without being offensive or rude. It helps if you can use the appropriate facial expressions. However, never fall for the obvious trap of over-explaining things to your subordinates or seniors. Simply say no the way you chose to, and be done with it.

Connect The Dots

There will be times where someone is seeking help with a task or an assignment from you, and you know of other people working on exactly the same type of work. Or when faced with a request for something you cannot do, if you know of a logical and feasible alternative, you can immediately direct the person towards the alternative. This is connecting the dots.

In such cases, not only is the problem resolved, but it is also resolved better than if you had done it.

- "Annual report? Have you checked with James? I believe he is working on that as well. You two might be working on the same assignment."
- "Gee! I am sorry, Tyler, but that's beyond my expertise – I don't know much about employment law. However, Rory in HR would be a good bet to ask."

Connecting the dots requires you to remain on top of your game. This is only possible if you are mindful of your surroundings and know exactly what is going on at that given time. If successful at dot connection, you will avoid any additional burden, and still get to help others out by connecting them with like-minded people. It is a classic example of a win-win situation.

Conversely, if you do help out with something you are not good at, then producing something shoddy could lose your professionalism, and the respect and trust of others. Sometimes it just doesn't pay to help!

Rain Check – *yes, but not now*

Sometimes, you want to say yes, not because you feel obliged but because you genuinely wish to help the person out. However, your current situation is already keeping you busy, and there is no room for any additional requests to come your way at the moment. Asking for a rain check is a great " way out" you can use. For those who don't know, a rain check is putting off activity to a later date – it's not saying no, in fact, it could be quite the opposite as you might be very positive about the idea. But you can't commit at this time because of other priorities.

For instance: did you receive an email or a text from a friend suggesting a catch-up? Or you may be working on an important assignment when suddenly your phone rings. It's your close friend, Amy.

"Hey Jessica! The girls and I have decided to meet up for a quick trip to the local mall. I will not take no for an answer, so you better be there."

Well, even before you could explain how busy you are, you have been barred from saying no. Despite this, you always have the choice to say no; begin by showing your interest in the other party's request, and that you agree it is a good idea. This builds rapport. Express that you'd love to come to the mall, but explain that you are working on something extremely important, and now it isn't convenient. Then ask for a raincheck and let them know you will miss not being there with them.

"Amy, I'd love to come, and I don't like giving you no for an answer, but can I take a raincheck and have lunch at the mall sometime next week. I'd love to see you, but I can't make it today at all."

Interested, But No Or Not Right Now!

Another strategy similar to the Rain Check is showing interest but being more definite about your unavailability. So the rain check response of "That sounds interesting; I'd love to do it but can't now." becomes "That sounds interesting; I'd love to do it, but I'm doing to have to decline." Or an even simpler response is "I'd love to, but not right now." No-one is going to be offended if you approach it this way.

Nothing Personal

Sometimes, people have a tendency to make everything personal. I knew a person who was assigned the duties of a quality assurance officer. It is the nature of their job to find flaws and point them out in the monthly evaluation report. I once was talking to the person, and I couldn't help but ask how he could carry on doing that, knowing that his job duties would only cause others to have a very negative image of him. His response is what got me thinking.

"I always tell them that it is a part of my duty and that it is nothing personal."

It is an excellent way to reiterate the fact that you are only performing the duties expected of you, and that there is nothing personal involved in the matter. At times, you may be facing situations where you will need to let others know what you cannot or would not do is nothing but a matter of professionalism and being fair to everyone else.

These are often quite tricky and challenging moments. These can certainly cause you to feel intimidated, but remember that it is only a part of what you do. Without over-explaining your situation, you can easily say no to what cannot be done, and the other person would understand, and move on. There is no need to feel under pressure. Your job or your priorities at home take precedence, and you are only doing what is best for absolutely everyone, even if that means saying no.

Say Yes To Part Of It

When you commit to helping part of the request, it shows the other person that you are willing to help and makes it easier for you to say no to the other part of the request.

Still remember the case with Liam and Rick at the beginning of this book? Let's assume that Rick told Liam to help him log in and get the work left done and submitted since it is due in one hour.

If you were Liam, you could say that "Hey Rick, I can help you log in for sure but I have some work that is due in one hour too, so I don't think I have time for yours". Rick will still not be 100% happy with it, but there is little room for him to complain since you already promised to help him log in.

Short And Concise

Not all situations require you to be friendly. You may be a manager in a firm or the disciplinarian in the family. Order must be followed to ensure everyone contributes to their roles. If you see someone approaching you for an extra favor, you can keep things as simple as possible and just say:

"I am sorry, but no!"

Remain quiet after saying that, and give a firm look. This should immediately end the conversation. Yes, it would be a bit awkward, but everyone has to do this at some point in their life, whether as an individual or a professional.

Safety Phrase – when all else fails

You are doing your own thing when all of a sudden, a request pops in. You are not prepared, and you do not have any time to think up a way to deny the request. This is where your safety phrase can come to the rescue. Great safety words are "maxed-out" or "no capacity right now". It's handy to have these prepared and up your sleeve, but please remember this is not a license to lie. Remain honest, use the safety phrase, and let the other party know you cannot possibly help right now. Who knows, the other party may be able to help you out to ease your burden for a change.

SAYING NO WITHOUT SAYING NO

It is a useful strategy to say no without actually saying no. Confused? Let me explain this one with a little example.

Not so long ago, I had a friend who worked in a customer service department at one of the leading megastores in the US. His job was to look after customers and provide them with after-sales services. Naturally, dealing in such a department comes with the risk of facing irate customers.

To handle such tough customers, my friend was trained to say no without saying no. It is no surprise that people being told 'no' can often feel humiliated, provoked, or even angry. To avoid falling into such situations, he was trained to use other words such as:

"I am so sorry to hear that, and I wish I was able to help out more in this matter."

"Can I offer you anything else?"

If you think about it, these are just another way of saying no, but these stand a better chance of being accepted. The second response is a bit tricky, and we will discuss that a little later.

The beauty of it is that my friend wasn't even lying. He knows the values his company follows, he knows the boundaries under which they can operate, and hence he never lies and still manages to deny claims which fall outside the coverage with ease.

There are a million ways through which you can say no, but not all of them allow you to speak the truth. Avoid making excuses or lying when you are saying no. It is quite possible that you may have told someone else something, forgotten about it, and then repeated the same thing to someone else on a completely different day. If luck has it, and these two parties were to interact with each other, they may actually discuss how you refused them and find out that you only made up stories.

The Silent Treatment

This is not an ideal strategy, but it is worth knowing about. It could be summed up by "You have the right to remain silent."

There may be times where you know saying no would cause more harm than good. You also know that you cannot say yes because that too will cause issues of unimaginable scale. The best way to go about it is to remain silent.

Silence can often be quite clear to show what you wish to say. The silence shows your disappointment and discomfort towards a particular issue. You can face such issues at home when the kids are upsetting the family, and your partner decides to ground them. Giving a silent answer would show that you are not thrilled by their actions either and that you were clearly not expecting them to behave in such a way. It also shows them that you are disappointed that it came down to this, but you tend to agree with the outcome—an easier way but one that is not the most enjoyable.

Stick to the truth and either find a way to communicate the truth in a calm and composed manner or learn more effective methods of saying no. One such method is to use the phrase "not right now" when presented with additional work.

Neither Yes Nor No

Life brings us face to face with various situations, and some may be trickier to fully understand right away. When you find yourself in such a situation, always try and gain as much time as you can to fully understand what needs to be done and whether or not you should do it.

"I will have to think about this one. I will get back to you once I know what needs to be done."

With such lines, you are giving some hope and still not disappointing the other person. After some deliberation, you can let them know whether it is worth your while or expertise, or if you would let it pass.

Saying No To Yourself!

Practicing saying no to others can help you learn to say no to yourself, which will also reflect on your finances and savings.

By knowing when to say no to your own spending, you save a lot more than you normally would. I have seen people who keep saying no to pretty much everything, and initially, it didn't make any sense to me. It was only after a couple of years that I realized how much their savings grew just by refusing to spend it lavishly on cars, decorative items, gadgets, etc.

Saying no takes time, practice, and a bit of willpower. After your first no, you will start gaining all that almost immediately. You will see the results sooner than you can expect, and things will start changing all around you. Do not be intimidated. Simply prepare yourself for the change and enjoy as things start to grow simpler.

IN SUMMARY

It will take some practice, but once you learn how to say no, things will start getting a lot easier for you and those around you. Now, everyone will know whether they can bother you with a certain task or not. All those annoying requests which previously added to your burden will now cease to exist.

Think back to Rick bothering Liam in the Introduction. Now imagine Rick getting this text in response to his persistent requests.

"Hey Rick! I am sorry but I will not be covering you. It would be unfair for the rest if I continue to cover you like I did

before. I hope things turn out OK for you and you find a way to get the work done."

That should end the never-ending string of texts which always asked Liam to cover for him. I assure you, Rick or whoever "Rick" is in your life, would only feel embarrassed after reading such a text. You've carefully stated your views, but you have also given them a chance to improve their own ways and put in the effort, just like everyone else.

When you go on to refuse others by saying no, directly or otherwise, always expect some push-back – it might not come, but be ready for it. When it does come, remain resilient and true to your principles, core values, and boundaries. Eventually, everyone will get the message and not bother you with the same type of request again.

It is also something that would open doors for you in the future. As someone who takes care of the house, you would earn more respect and set examples for others to follow, whether that is your husband, wife, sons, or daughters. It will allow you to be an example for the neighbors as well.

This chapter gave you some well-tested methods to learn how to say no. Keeping your values, boundaries and priorities in sight, things should now start to seem a little easier for you. Practice saying no, or better yet, make it a personal goal to say no a few times every day. The more you practice, the greater your confidence will be, and it is only with confidence that you can become assertive. Otherwise, you will find yourself requested frequently to do things you do not wish to do.

Now that you know some strategies of saying no, it is now time to move on and learn the 'how' behind it all. You will need to use the right tone, the right facial and body expressions, and much more to further help you communicate your message easily. The next chapter will teach you exactly that.

6

HOW TO DELIVER THE NO MESSAGE

First of all, congratulations on learning perhaps the most important aspect of the book – what to say when saying no, and equally importantly, what not to say. Hopefully, by now, you've managed your first no, and that all went well for you. However, just saying no is not always enough. To be more successful, you need to learn HOW you should say it. The difference to the previous chapter is that it focused on what the message should be, whereas now we focus on how the message is presented. This is our body language, our vocal tone, and even our facial expressions.

You've made great progress in learning your lines, knowing what needs to be said in a variety of situations. At this point, most people now simply hope that all will be well in a difficult situation. However, this isn't always the case. For a lot of people, when situations don't work out the way they had hoped for, they feel confused and revert back to the old dialog habits. The obvious mistake they make is focusing only on *what* to say and not *how* to say it. In Chapter 5, we focused on the words to say, the overt message. Now, in Chapter 6, we'll look at the less overt side of the message – the non-verbal messages that accompany the spoken words.

This chapter will walk you through some important tips and suggestions, tried and tested to work in almost all situations. You already know what words to say in your given situation –

now learn how to gain the edge you need to convey your message respectfully and clearly. You'll see how interrelated the non-verbal cues are, and although we deal with them slightly differently, it should be clear that to adjust one is to adjust the overall message.

EXPRESSIONS AND STANCE

These cover the physical behaviors to make when saying no. In the next "Tones and Emotions" section, we'll cover matters relating to how your voice sounds.

If you were paying close attention to the previous chapter, you will have noticed that we could come across situations where we either paused or remained silent. Even though there is no verbal communication, we are still conveying messages through our expressions and our posture. The styles and methods of presentation are as important as the words being spoken. Behaviouralists believe that up to 70% of a message is communicated non-verbally.

So, what messages are we conveying? Let's look at a few examples where you remain silent AND do one of the following:

- Look downcast at the floor OR
- You stare aggressively at the person OR
- You sneer at them OR
- You shake your head repeatedly and shrug your

shoulders OR
- You regard them calmly, without antagonism.

Although there is no verbal message, there is still some message that is delivered loud and clear:

- In looking downcast, you come across as submissive, which is to invite reaction.
- Staring aggressively provokes anger and hostility.
- Sneering denigrates or ridicules the recipient. Who wants to feel that?
- Shaking your head and shrugging denotes exasperation
- Being calm implies internal authority, a strong response.

Now, to be clear, I'm not suggesting that you take some of the more negative approaches outlined above; I'm simply showing that different physical body positions and expressions can influence the message you're trying to deliver and could have lasting implications for any future relationship you have with that particular person. Ensure then that you use the appropriate body language to further instill how serious you are.

In all situations, retain respect for the person with whom you are dealing, even if this is difficult. Maintain eye contact, avoid looking away or shifting your gaze repeatedly, and use a firm voice to reflect your desire or disapproval about things. You can use appropriate hand gestures where necessary to further stress key points that you wish to convey. This will build trust and help to draw that person to you during what could be a difficult conversation. At all times, make the non-verbal messages as clear as the verbal ones so that the overall message is not diluted with conflicting cues – if you're *saying* no, but nodding, that's a conflict that will cause confusion.

In general, the approach to take is one of calm assertiveness with an open stance and arms held in a non-threatening way.

TONES AND EMOTIONS

This section covers the way words are actually spoken. Did you know in 2002, a study of surgeons found a clear link between surgeons who spoke calmly and with authority during office visits with patients and lower rates of malpractice claims history? Where tone and emotion were elevated, surgeons had a greater malpractice claims history. Now perhaps this just means that surgeons who really know what they are doing are also secure in themselves, which naturally translates into a calmer demeanor. However, that's not what the evidence was suggesting. Instead, it seemed to imply that just by communicating authority, they raised trust levels in their patients to a statistically significant level. Incredibly, tone and the emotion behind it are really critical to successful outcomes.

Think back to some of the emails and text messages you've received where you thought the tone of the message was one thing, but you found out later it was a completely different thing. Those written forms of communication where there is no ancillary information about the message, such as vocal tone, are notorious for the wrong message being delivered. If you don't believe me, read a few messages from friends or your partner, adding an angry tone to it. What did you get out of the message? Now go back to the same message and read it with a happy and calm tone. Almost certainly, you got a different message from exactly the same words that you read just moments ago. This shows how important the tone, or the lack of it, can influence how the message is received.

Being Courteous And Assertive

Courtesy is what allows you to save your reputation, respect, and image in the eyes of the other party. Saying no to anyone now shouldn't burn your bridges with them – remember, you may very well need this person's assistance in the future. By being rude or blunt, yes, you save yourself now, but at the cost of closing future doors inside which a good relationship with them might have opened.

Remain courteous while saying no. A polite approach will normally ensure that the message is received well and that no one feels offended. However, being courteous does not mean you should let your guard down either, or becoming submissive. In fact, it is a sign of strength to remain calm in the face of an offended person. Do your best to remain assertive, maintaining control of the conversation.

"Right now, I am already jumbled up. I would be lying if I said I could help at this point. Perhaps in the future, I will let you know if I can help."

Assertive, in control, and polite. The message is instantly clear.

Remaining Gracious

This is an important one, and exercising this will allow you to maintain a healthy relationship even after saying no. Whether it is a friend, a member in the house, or someone at work, whenever you must say no, do so in a gracious manner. Your approach to the situation would decide the outcome. A "no" will always serve as a blow, but it depends on your behavior, which decides how soft or harsh the blow will be.

Avoid Being A Pushover

Some people tend to push others over and over again. When saying no, ensure that you do not become a pushover. Talk about it in the most concise and simplest manner, and end the discussion. There is no need to apologize again and again, as this may portray a negative image. You can lose your self-esteem, and people around you would also lose their respect for you. Once you have made a decision, stick to it and let things run their natural course. Should the asker become rude or pushy, then you should become more firm because you are the one who makes decisions for you, not others. Thus, avoid being a pushover and stand firm so that others don't manipulate or bully you into giving an answer you don't want to give.

Tackling The Blame Game

Now you've delivered your message. You've stated quite clearly that the answer is No. However, the person to whom you are speaking has potentially taken offense and may begin passing comments or judgments on you and might even start blaming you for being rude and unhelpful. When caught in such situations, do not let such acts get to you. It is important to take the high road here: understand that if someone cannot accept no as an answer, it is most likely the problem rests with them, not with you. We will deal with this more in detail in Chapter 7.

IN SUMMARY

Communication is as much how a message is delivered as what the message actually is, and the non-verbal ones often deliver powerful ancillary messages. When we are saying no, be mindful of our tone of voice, posture, body language, and emotions. All of these have to work to complement each other. Get one of these wrong, and a different message will be received on the other end.

While we have learned how to say No, there is still something that can catch you off-guard unless you prepare yourself for certain tactics that others deliberately use to delay matters or push back. You will learn how to handle these in the next chapter.

7

THE TACTICS OF DIFFICULT PEOPLE AND HOW TO DEAL WITH THEM

This chapter will help you deal with some of the tougher cases you might face. Not everyone will accept your answer for how it is. There would be some who would push back, try to negotiate with you, or even act agitated upon hearing an answer they were not ready to hear. As a person who is trying to bring a much-needed change, you will need to know how to tackle such situations without letting down your boundaries, your guard, and your values.

This chapter will be brief, but the information discussed in this chapter should provide you with ample examples and situations to understand what needs to be done. Remember, it will take some practice before you fully grasp the confidence and method of saying no to the toughest customers, literally or otherwise.

KNOWING THEIR TACTICS

Sometimes, you may feel like a person is getting on your nerves. You may be tempted to lose your temper and tell them to shut up. However, that isn't a part of what we are trying to learn here. Doing so will cause you to lose your respect with the other party and possibly around others as well. As an individual, a friend, or even a professional, we must follow our values and norms just as we expect others to do so.

Remember the golden rule in life, which has always helped me calm down in tough situations. If you wish to be treated kindly, treat others kindly first. Even in the most demanding situations, learn how to control your temper and emotions. Do not let your emotions dictate how you would act. By remaining focused, calm, and clear of any emotional barricades, you stand a better chance to fully understand what the other person wants to say. You can then make an informed decision and either say yes or say no without offending them.

People often try to come up with the vaguest of excuses and reasons to convince you. Their objective is to gain favor, some kind of advantage, or at times assistance to sort out their matters and assignments. I am not suggesting that this is the case every time. Sometimes, people genuinely approach you with pure intentions. They do so to seek guidance and help. This is why it is necessary that you familiarize yourself with certain tactics that would allow you to differentiate between those who deserve your time and those who just want to take advantage of you.

Tactics Often Used By Organizations And Merchants

Where it is good, a hint of evil will also lurk. Someone I know has been a part of an organization where they would ask everyone for donations and subtly (and not so subtly!) force their employees to pay more than they felt comfortable paying.

It is wise that you keep an eye out and only do what you are comfortable with. If you come across people gathering money or someone telling you that most have chipped in a specific amount, let them know if this amount is feasible or if you cannot chip in straight away. Once again, there is no point in stretching this discussion longer. Avoid peer pressure and maintain control of your own savings and earnings.

This is also something to note because you will often find yourself in situations where you really wish to cancel a gym membership or a cable service, or perhaps even say no to a fundraising event because you already have plans involving your finances. These are tricky to deal with, especially given the fact that members of such events or organizations are brimming with the power to convince you to retain the membership or service or make a significant donation. For example, they may offer you a discounted membership price to make you stay. They may even tell you that they are heartbroken to hear that you want to cancel their service to make you feel guilty. If you are not prepared for those tactics, you are likely to change your no to a yes.

It is vital that you stand your ground and respectfully deny the services or the opportunity to donate. From the previous chapters, you already know what you need to say, and if you have been following this chapter closely, you would now have a better idea of how to say it.

Vague Information

Always ask what exactly it is you are being asked to do. Most of the time, the other party would give you vague information or talk about things that are completely irrelevant. Sometimes, this is simply to make it sound less challenging a task than it actually is. Once you're involved, it becomes harder for you to say no. Unknown to them, you are asking questions not because you are interested in knowing what the work is about; instead, you are asking the question to find out what their true intention is. For example, if somebody asks you to help him/her move. You may want to ask him/her a couple of questions like: "Will you make sure to get your stuff packed before I come?"; "How many people will be helping you move?"; "How long will it take?". This can save you from doing the work that he/she could have done before moving and spending much more time than you planned.

It is common to find people giving you vague information. This is especially true if you are investing in a property, getting a membership at some gym or sports center, or even trying to buy a used car. This is a deliberate action, and it is carried out to obscure and hide away anything that may push you to think otherwise and walk away from the deal. Always be mindful of what you are looking at and try to ask specific questions. Remember, it is your choice to go for something or not, which is the reason why you do not want to let your decisions be influenced by the charming salesman or an eager seller who is clearly all-praises about something they may be selling.

Asking them questions like "Why are you selling this?" would be a perfect way to get started if you are unable to find any flaws. Clearly, people re-sell items when they neither need them nor are able to restore them in working condition. Ask the right questions. If possible, bring someone who may be a bit of an expert to help you make the right decisions.

Constant Interruptions

When someone wants to dominate you, they will resort to talking over you, interrupting your responses on purpose to reinforce their will. If you come across such situations, remain calm, and remember all that I have said before. Be an active listener and hear them out completely. Once they have finished, resume what you were trying to say in the first place. The look on their faces is often priceless!

"I see. While I am sure you are trying to do what is best for you, I too must do what is best for me. At this point, I cannot help you with your task, but I certainly hope you find what you are looking for."

It seems more like a piece of dialogue from a movie, but it is mighty effective.

Borrowing

We may all have experiences with people who just do not know when to stop borrowing money. It seems they always need money for something, which is always important. They promise they will return you the money, but when you ask them to pay you back, they lose their temper and behave erratically.

People borrow money from those whom they think would not mind lending at all. They specifically try to target people who are either making a significant amount of money or will not mind if the repayment gets a bit delayed. They would approach you and try to make things sound urgent, but they would never provide you with clear answers. Then, there are some who, just like Mark from my friend Peter's experience, would propose brilliant investment ideas and convince you to be a partner.

Make it a policy not to lend money to anyone—friends or family members alike. With whoever approaches you with a brilliant business idea or an urgent need of cash, be honest and concise. Here are a few good answers you can use to divert such issues away.

"I am sorry, but I don't lend money to anyone. I've seen good friendships ruined by it and I rather like you as a friend."

And if it's for a business venture: *"I'm sorry, I'm just not qualified to know whether that's a good or bad investment – I don't have the experience in that field to make a good judgment."* After all, that is the genuine reason that investors on TV programs like Shark Tank use before bowing out of the running.

. . .

Taking Unusual Interest

When someone is trying to win a favor or two from you, or seek your help with their own tasks, they may resort to some unusual tactics. Normally, you may have noticed people engaged with their own work, but just when they feel like you are the sort of person they can convince to help, they would pour in an endless supply of how brilliant you are. They would praise the quality of work you do and how efficient you can be.

Do not give in to these. Remain composed and true to your work because what's about to come next is a request that you already know you will say no to.

"Jim, while I appreciate you paying attention to my work, I would like to continue working. If you do need help, I know someone who might be able to assist you."

You can direct such a co-worker to your superiors or someone who is tasked to assist others.

DEALING WITH THE DIFFICULT ONES

Above were some of the most common tactics used at home, between friends, and at work. However, what if you really bump into someone who just refuses to take no for an answer, and is constantly stepping into your space to ask for help nonetheless? How do you deal with such people?

"Well, I can report them."

True. You can report them, but that is if they are someone you work with. What if this person is your boss or a client? In such situations, you need to know how to handle the situation and gain the upper hand. Follow these simple steps, and even the toughest customer would eventually give in, and you get to maintain your boundaries without giving way to any drama.

1. **Listen** - Even though the next person may be the world's most annoying co-worker or friend, it is best to stay calm and hear them out first.
2. **Remain calm** - Regardless of what they have to say, do not lose your composed stature.
3. **Do not rush to judge** - No one likes to be judged, and the same should be applicable here. Do not judge them immediately. Instead, give them a chance to speak their mind.
4. **Respect their views** - Whatever it may be that they have to say, show respect. Sometimes, your show of respect can cause the other party to cool off and apologize.
5. **Seek out the intent** - There is always a need or an intention behind all the drama and the constant nagging. Try to find out what exactly that is. If you can get to the root of the cause, you can immediately redirect the entire conversation.
6. **Do not demand compliance** - Just because someone is mad or clearly disturbed, do not tell them

to calm down immediately. This may only cause the other person to go irate. Instead, ask what seems to bother them.

7. **Do not say "I understand"** - Saying "I understand" will only make matters worse. Instead, try "Tell me more so that I can understand better."
8. **No smiling matter** - Of course, smiling at such an odd moment would both be inappropriate and downright offending. Ensure that you use the right body language for the situation. Remain attentive and allow the other party to share their concerns.
9. **No need to defend** - Despite what the other person may have to say, there is no point in going all defensive. This person is clearly in an emotional state and may not be thinking straight.
10. **Keep anger out of it** - They may have some harsh words to say, but do not respond to anger with anger. Use a low, calm, and concerned tone to re-establish peace.
11. **Try not to argue** - Easier said than done, but if you remain quiet, there is a good chance the other person would calm down quickly.
12. **Maintain extra space** - In such situations, it is best to keep some extra distance and avoid touching the other person. It is observed in some cases that people tend to pat the other person on the shoulders or the back, and this signal is often misinterpreted.

13. **Reassure the other person** - By saying you will look into the matter or have it resolved can often go a very long way. You do not necessarily have to do this on your own, you can always link this person with someone who can help, and you still get to feel good.
14. **Debrief the situation** - When the time is right, summarize what you heard and let them know what can or will be done.
15. **Allow your own stress to flow out** - Sure enough, you held all that stress in. It is time to let it go. Take a walk or go for a run. Keep your nerves and head calm and clear.
16. **Give yourself credit** - A pat on the back or a quick treat is the need of the hour. You just tackled an incredibly tough situation.

Handling clients or bosses can often be tough. They may use words that may be harsh to hear to manipulate you into giving a better deal or take on more responsibility than you can manage, but once you learn how to tackle such situations, you would soon be climbing the ladder of success faster than you could have ever imagined before. Not only will people start noticing you, but they will approach you to teach them how you do what you do.

Lead as a role model for others and be the person everyone wishes to follow. To maintain that place and respect, never let your boundaries or guard be compromised because, as soon as you do, you are back to square one, and everyone would immediately start ignoring you.

So how do we avoid backsliding? We will look at some of the most common mistakes people make when they are trying to say no. Such issues would lead to confusion and might even break their newly gained confidence right away. It is necessary that you familiarize yourself with these and ensure that you avoid walking into the obvious errors for maximum results.

8

COMMON ISSUES TO AVOID WHEN SAYING NO

Learning any new skills brings you the likelihood to make mistakes. That is, after all, the whole point of learning. We err to a greater or less degree naturally when we try new things even though we wish to do things right. The outcome of these mistakes, however small or large they were, can be profound.

This chapter will help you learn to recognize the signs of key mistakes that people make when saying no, so that you can avoid all of them and say No without inviting trouble in your way. You have already learned how to say No and how to determine whom to say No to. Now let's look at some of the most common mistakes out there. We'll identify them, understand them, and then we can avoid them in real-life situations.

THE SEVEN MOST COMMON MISTAKES

Almost everyone who has just learned how to say No would love to go out there and start making changes to their lives. However, before you rush to experience how it feels, pay attention to these errors and see how these can ruin your plan instantly.

1. **Over-explaining** – This was mentioned in Chapter 5 but still needs to be emphasized here. People tend to give in to the temptation of explaining all of their reasons for why they are saying no. Over-explaining portrays doubt, regret, and might even cause the other person to misinterpret your explanations as an excuse. Therefore always be concise and to the point.
2. **Waiting to say no** – you are now strategically poised to say No. You've done all the training, and you're just waiting for the right opportunity. But there are two big unknowns in this situation: we don't know when the first chance will actually arrive, and we don't know what our emotional response will be, or how the exchange will affect us. Instead of waiting, be proactive. Find situations that you can start to say No to immediately, ones that don't require the input of others, for example: "No work over the weekend" or "No more hanging out at the bar." Find these no's and get them sorted out in your head now. Then when

someone says, "Would you mind working over the weekend?" you've already thought through that situation and can calmly reply that you can't.

3. **Being vague** – coherence and clarity are signs of an effective communicator. When saying no, be sure to communicate clearly. Do not leave room for doubts using phrases like "kind of" or "sort of."
4. **Hoping for approval** – you have just said no to somebody. This "No" is a decision of yours that has been approved by you; thus, there is no need to seek others' approval. Seeking approval shows others your unassertiveness and will unintentionally hint that you may say yes if others insist on their requests.
5. **Hollow promises** – these are promises made despite knowing you can't deliver on them. Don't do this! This can tarnish your reputation, lower the esteem with which you are held, and possibly cause the next mistake: guilt.
6. **Allowing guilt** – guilt is slippery. It slides in and undermines your footing, destabilizing your position. If your footing becomes unbalanced and you become flustered, you will struggle to hold to your stated no, altering your response to a yes instead. Be sure that no is what you mean to say, and if you are sure, then be prepared not to be "guilted" into changing your decision.
7. **Try to Avoid** – we can become people who try to

avoid other people, avoid making eye contact, and even changing direction if they are heading our way. We do this and hope that the other party would understand we do not wish to talk to them about something. If anything, you are damaging your reputation and yourself as an individual. Instead, face the situation and say, "No, I can't" to resolve the situation.

These mistakes are not easy to avoid. The only way to be ready for them is to practice. Remember various scenarios in your life where they have already happened and, with the benefit of hindsight, work out what would have been a better response from your side at the time of the incident. Once you've worked through several of these, you should soon be more comfortable with expressing your views, and answering as you would like to, with ease.

A QUICK TASK: PRACTICE SAYING NO

Before you take on the real-life scenarios, it is best to familiarize yourself by practicing them. This would allow you to be fully prepared for almost all eventualities, hence giving you the upper hand. Remember, a prepared mind will always deliver better results than an unprepared one. Now that you know the 'what' and the 'how,' it is time to bring that all together and start practicing. As the old saying goes, "practice makes perfect".

Knowing the seven most common issues, write down at least three varied and unique scenarios that normally would leave you worried or concerned. Imagine the scenario and think about the stressors present at that moment in time. Familiarize yourself with those emotions and plan your response to them. Find what works best for you. Don't worry if you can't find these scenarios right away.

Practice on your own before you need to use these strategies in real life. Nothing does that better than a large mirror. If you truly wish to make the most of it, make it a habit to practice at least 3 minutes every day before stepping out of the house or engaging in other activities until you get comfortable doing it.

The first few tries might make you feel slightly uncomfortable and awkward, but once you get the hang of things, the results would start flowing. The objective is to practice your methods and learn how to positively use your interpersonal and communication skills.

Practice all the examples and scenarios which we learned earlier on. Practice saying these as if you were actually speaking to another person. Be confident, maintain eye contact, and use the appropriate tone to ensure maximum results. It also helps to record your audio or video to review how you did later on.

Make this a habit, and soon you will feel the difference. You will be more comfortable saying no to others, and you would automatically know if you used the right tone, the right kind of body language, and if you conveyed the message.

Speaking of scenarios, in the next chapter, we will walk through some real-life situations and scenarios to see how we can use all that we have learned to mitigate the issue. You are nearly there!

9

TIPS TO SAY NO BY SCENARIO

Every one of us faces unique scenarios and different challenges daily. It is hard to replicate the same scenario for everyone, if not impossible. However, there are certain scenarios that tend to be universal.

In this chapter, we will be going through some of these scenarios which can and will take place in life at some point in time. We will see how we can handle people around us and respond to them with a firm but respectful no. If it helps, write these down on a piece of paper and practice doing these in your spare time. The more you practice, the easier they will be to deliver.

Before I do move on, keep those answers/scenarios I asked you to identify in the previous chapter with you. It is time to find out how well you were able to manage things, given your current understanding. There is no right or wrong here, but the point behind the exercise is to allow you to compare and take notes throughout this chapter and see which additional strategies you can apply to make things a little easier for you.

THE SCENARIOS

Facing Co-Workers

We have already covered this in "Your Goals Matter" of Chapter 3; however, for revision, you will need to set out your plans for the day, week, month, or even the year. Prioritize these goals and objectives accordingly. By doing so, you know which of these short-term and long-term tasks require your maximum concentration. Only by knowing these thoroughly can you filter out requests from your co-workers and differentiate between the ones which must be helped and those that should be declined.

It is also helpful, and a good habit, to hear what your colleague has to say before you decide to say No. Let them finish their request in full. Then it's your turn – respond quickly and firmly. Do not drag the matter with unusual pauses. By hearing them out, you are giving them respect, and by answering quickly after they have finished, you are allowing them to seek other alternatives. If needed, provide a reason why you have turned the request down in a polite and friendly manner.

Quite a few companies provide employees with calendar applications, such as Outlook, Google Calendar, and others, which are synced to a common server. These calendars can provide information about the availability of any employees at any given time. If you have one as well, ensure you add some busy blocks every day. This would allow you to know when you need to focus and work hard. You can turn away all requests and distractions to ensure you go through the block with maximum productivity. It also helps if you can maintain a calendar with some available slots. These are ideal when asked what time you can hold a quick meeting. One simple glimpse, and you should have your answer right there.

Finally, you can print out your weekly schedule and keep it next to you and show just how much you have on your plate to your co-workers when they walk to your desk the next time for assistance. I have often gone to speak to a colleague with a request, seen their calendar is completely full, and refrained from asking them what I had originally planned to. It works!

Facing The Boss

I saved this deliberately for this chapter. Saying no to anyone else can be easy and manageable. There is not much to worry about except some occasional comments, which would generally fade with time. All we need to do is to remain persistent, and the rest will vanish. However, when it comes to the ultimate authority at your workplace, things are different.

For a second, close your eyes and imagine facing your boss. While most bosses are composed, to the point and calm, imagine your boss is the kind of person who is always looking for an excuse to lose their temper and lay someone off the job for even the slightest dip in quality or performance. This is the person who simply cannot take no for an answer. Everyone fears this person because, without his signature and approval, no one is getting paid or allowed to continue working. Surely, you cannot imagine saying no to this boss, can you?

As it turns out, there actually are ways you can do so. It completely depends on what kind of interaction and trust level you share with your boss. If you are someone who can crack a joke or two and still remain at ease, things may get a lot easier. However, if you are someone who always tries to look the other way when your boss walks past you, you will need all the confidence and critical thinking you can muster at that point in time.

It is eventually bound to happen, and you cannot avoid it either. There will come a time when you will need to let your boss know you cannot do something. Just thinking about it would give our mind a run for its money. We would start thinking of a million reasons to try and rationalize why we said no, right? That is where most people go wrong.

If you start making up excuses or rationalizing things unnecessarily, you are bound to say something wrong. Mind you, you are facing your boss, and there is every likelihood that your boss would figure out you are making excuses. Instead, stick to being honest.

Here is a typical example of how someone can say No to their boss without raising any alarms:

Person A: *"Thanks for thinking of me, Boss, but I am afraid I already have enough on my plate."*

Boss: *"So?"*

Person A: *"So, if I say yes to this, I know I would not be able to do justice to the task. I have enough workload as it is, and trying to squeeze this in would affect the overall quality of the work I am doing. I know I wouldn't be satisfied with the outcome, and that leaves me to wonder: if I am not satisfied, how can I expect you to feel any different about my work?"*

It is a perfect way to let your boss know that you genuinely care for the quality of the outcome, which is why you are letting them know of your current situation. You can also add that if any of the tasks are reassigned to lessen the burden, you can certainly have a go at this. It shows that you are not willing to compromise on the quality of the job and that you are also determined to work effectively.

The outcome of such a conversation would allow you to be noticed by your boss. They may also keep tabs on your performance. Naturally, this may frighten you, but if you continue to perform your duties with integrity, honesty, and devotion, you may just walk in one day to find a pleasant surprise.

Every company or corporation values a good employee, and they will always be willing to retain employees who can get the job done with quality and take responsibilities. By playing that vital role, you automatically become an important cog in the company's wheel without which a significant part of the operation will stop working.

Remember, when facing your boss, do not hold back the facts. Let them out in the open so that your boss can see the clear logic. Most bosses, regardless of how intimidating they may be, care about the facts and the results. If you can provide both of these, there is no reason for you to worry about what would happen if you say No. You would neither lose your job nor be demoted for explaining the situation as it was.

Here are some good ways to communicate and say No without actually saying no to your boss:

- Instead of saying you do not have time, try "If I take that on, can you help me to reprioritize the projects I am working on?
- By doing so, you not only bring your boss's attention to the fact that you are already filled with tasks, but you are also showing eagerness to work and take on challenges as they come along. Your boss would appreciate the fact that you seek their assistance for such matters.
- Instead of saying it won't work, use "Can I share another idea for discussion?"
- Sometimes, it is just wrong to say something can't be done. Your boss, just like you, is a human being. This means that the boss may start assuming you are not willing to work or even think out of the box. By presenting a possibility that there is another idea, your boss would likely hear you out. Who knows, this

may very well be the big break you needed all this time.
- Instead of saying you don't want to, "I would love to; however, I am already preoccupied with these assignments."
- Once again, you are letting your boss know how much work you have. It is possible that you may have the specific set of skills the task requires, and if it is urgent, your boss might just be able to transfer the workload to someone else while providing you with something worth your time to work on.

Further tips are presented for saying no to the boss:

- Always provide a valid reason
- Have an alternative solution
- Show them you appreciate being thought of for the task
- Nominate or find someone else who can get the job done
- Always be empathetic
- If possible, buy yourself a bit of time
- No point in beating around the bush
- Always acknowledge who is in charge
- End the conversation firmly and professionally
- Do not take anything personally
- Be sure to set healthy boundaries

- Analyze your boss's mood before you speak
- Be in the boss's shoes and think from their perspective

Unlike anyone else, your boss is someone who is paying you to work for them, or if a manager in a larger company, then they influence annual appraisal ratings, which may have an impact on your income. They must be treated with respect for their position and years of experience. However, this does not mean that they can't be wrong. There are times you may have a lot riding on your shoulders, and at such times, you will need to communicate this to them.

Find out the right time to talk to your boss or manager. If they are in a receptive mood, be sure to talk clearly and confidently. If it is urgent, it is always safe to send an email first and await their response. If they are interested in hearing you out, let them know the issue right away.

Facing Clients

Clients can be a bit less intimidating than our bosses, but they too can often be hard to say no to. We already covered some bases when it comes to dealing with clients when talking about "Dealing with the Difficult ones" in chapter 7. However, to further ease matters for you, here are some tips to ensure you know exactly how to say no and what to do when you have done so:

- Begin by thanking them before responding with a no

- Remain transparent and explain why you cannot fulfill the request
- Follow up about referrals
- Share content that is helpful with clients
- Ensure you remain connected to them to the best of your abilities
- When you can fulfill their requests, reach out to them right away
- If something is not feasible, soften the blow politely with a counterproposal

Clients are the source of revenue and business for any firm or organization. Dealing with them takes quite a lot of practice, patience, and confidence.

When dealing with clients, always know what you need to speak about. Never indulge in matters which are anything but business.

HANDLING THE ONES WE CARE ABOUT

Your Spouse

Ah! This is where things can get a bit tricky. Now, we are talking about people we truly care about, and that changes almost everything. How can you say no to them? Well, you have already learned most of it. However, here are some great steps which can help you to say no without causing an issue for yourself or your spouse:

- Acknowledge whatever their wish is
- Avoid vagueness— just as we learned previously, we need to ensure we do not provide vague explanations this time
- Add something positive to the mix to ease any tension
- Take turns—listen first, talk, then repeat.
- Avoid the argument
- Respond appropriately – use the right tone, right posture, right words to maintain a healthy discussion. Do not let bouts of anger and irritation get the better of you.

In most cases, this should easily allow you to resolve the issue without getting into unnecessary debates and heated drama, which needs to be avoided as much as possible.

Children

Ok, when it comes to children, I could write a whole book on setting boundaries with them. Parents are often more permissive than necessary with their kids in the hope of building friendships with them, and so the children don't grow up holding grudges against their parents who seemed unsupportive by always saying no. Just remember though you are the main guide in their lives and setting boundaries will always do them more good than harm.

So don't be afraid to say No, but where possible, provide them with productive distractions. These would normally end the entire situation peacefully. When you see them doing something good, appreciate them and praise them. This motivates them to do things better. Start by imposing a single limit. Let them know when they step over the line. Once they understand, introduce another, and so on.

Do not give them hollow promises, or unrealistic consequences — ones that you cannot deliver. They will remember that for years to come. Do not fall for manipulative talk and try to understand the real goal behind such flattery. Most of these would ensure that your children remain in line with your values and goals.

Friends And Neighbors

We already know how important they are. Perhaps, if you have been following the previous chapters, you would have a good idea of how to handle them when the time comes, and you need to say no. However, I am not ready to leave you with vagueness either, which is why I decided to provide you with a few productive ways to make saying no a little easier and still be on good speaking terms. The last part is important as quite often; people forget that words can hurt others rather easily.

- Be receptive and eager to hear them out
- Find out all the details and filter out the irrelevant information
- Where possible, apologize before or after saying no
- Show them that you care and that you are understanding
- Clarify boundaries and set limits from the start. You cannot expect to do it later on and hope that your friends and neighbors will accept that. We covered this in Chapter 3.

By practicing saying no based on the scenarios above, you should be able to navigate some of life's trickier aspects with relative ease and confidence. Before we look at the final chapter of the book, I want you to go through the previous exercises from "Practicing Saying No" in Chapter 6 and "A Quick Task" in Chapter 8, then review your answers and modify or update the ones you answered previously. See how they differ with what you've learned since first writing them.

In the final chapter, we will look into how all of this can help you realize a life that you never thought existed. We will find out just how much we have been missing out on and how we can further enhance our experiences.

10

YOUR LIFE WITH THE POWER OF SAYING NO

Steve Jobs was known for being assertive, confident, and the kind of leader who would say no without second thoughts if he knew something was not worth his time. While some of the success that Apple enjoyed during Jobs' time was because of the revolutionary products, most of the success came because of Steve Jobs and his personality, style, and assertiveness that moved the audience and gained such a massive success. We all know that he is a talented and creative thinker, which builds his success, but he would not be as successful as he was without his assertiveness to say no to things that don't matter to him.

We may not found a company as great as Apple is, but we can be sure to improve our life with the power of saying no. Throughout the book, especially the first two chapters, we learned just how much we sacrifice if we do not have the confidence and ability to say No when we need to. There is no point in living a life where you are always the people pleaser because eventually, depression, anxiety, and other mental issues might get to you. You may feel that not a single soul in the world cares about what you want, and you would have no one else but yourself to blame.

Whatever the sacrifices you may have made so far, they are already enough. It is time to draw the line and lead with assertiveness, authority, and a clear vision from here on out.

I do not need to remind anyone of how difficult life was before you started to gain the confidence to say No, but what I can tell you is how great of a life you can expect to lead moving forward.

THE BENEFITS OF SAYING NO

By saying no freely, independently, and confidently, here are some highlights you can expect:

- A sharper focus on your important matters
- Make space for tougher assignments for yourself
- Gain more free time to rejuvenate
- Become a better, more honest friend
- Be an effective communicator
- Be a terrific partner
- Be an ideal co-worker
- Feel good about yourself
- Gain purpose and meaning
- Know yourself better

The benefits of saying no are only limited by your own imagination. The kind of life which we envy is exactly the type of life you will lead once you start taking control of your own life.

Saying no is not just conveying your honest thoughts; it is a complete art: one that many want, but only a few learn.

It is your passport to freedom of a different kind. Not only do you feel happier in life, but you become a better decision-maker and hence become more successful as a person, as an individual, and as a businessperson. Whether you were struggling to say No to yourself or those whom you care for, all it takes is a bit of practice and willpower, and the rest is just smooth sailing.

Remember all that you learned and ensure you put it to good use. Without practice, this book would serve you no good. I wish you only the best and hope that the only time you look back is to remind yourself how this moment went on to change your life for the better, permanently.

It will be really appreciated if you could take just 60 seconds to write a brief review on Amazon, even if it's just a few sentences!

CONCLUSION

Life is strange. It makes us say yes to things we don't wish to do, and then it stops providing us the confidence to say No when we desperately try to. For ages, men and women have struggled to find some definitive way to learn how to say No without ever feeling guilty of ruining someone else's day. Even if they may have come across such information, they just struggled with the idea of facing the guilt that seemingly fills their heart and makes them want to curse themselves. Why?

While we continue to say yes to almost everyone and everything, the people who say No are clearly leading a better lifestyle than us. We go through all the hard work and put in extra effort to help our dear friend, yet our friend, who clearly remains worry-free, is being promoted. How is that fair?

It is time to change things for ourselves. Clearly, this "yes sir" approach is leading us nowhere. We need to change our tactics, adopt a different kind of persona, and develop a plan through which we can regain control of our lives. We definitely need to learn what it is that others do, which allows them to remain at ease and unphased even when they have said no to so many souls just within an hour. Fortunately, this book provides all the information one would need to get started on the right track.

Master of The Arts: Excel Saying No is not just a book that points out the obvious. It is a complete guide that takes everyone through a journey to self-discovery. Through this journey, everyone can get to reconnect with their inner goals, core values, and rediscover that powerful person within them that subsided over time.

This book brings forth some of the most tried and tested methods to teach everyone how to get back on top, regain control of life and gain enough confidence to make some of the wisest decisions with ease. Guilt is just our perception; what lies beyond that is a greater reward than we never knew.

By learning and mastering how to say No, you get to live a completely different life. Not only do you become a better communicator, but you also go on to become a role model for many, a better partner, and definitely a better friend. You get to choose what to say yes to and what to decline.

This book teaches some of the science behind how saying no affects us. It also lists down some of the easiest ways for beginners to learn and apply in order to say No. It also discussed various scenarios and provided examples, tips, and suggestions on how to handle such situations, say No, and still come out victorious.

Practicing is the key, and we have done the mirror routine. Remember, the more you hone your skills, the better and more confident your delivery will be. If you picked this book to truly change your life, I assure you that you now have all the knowledge you need to do that. How and when you apply this knowledge is your call and yours alone.

I love helping people, it is a part of my life, and I thoroughly enjoy that. I would definitely love to know how I was able to help you and how this book contributed to your life. I will be keeping an eye out for your feedback and hope to find out that you are leading better lives than you once did. Your feedback is what will drive me to do more for everyone.

I wish you the best of luck wherever you may be. We are all human beings, and we make mistakes. It is only after committing mistakes that we gain a chance to learn, correct ourselves, and rise again better than before. I wish you find your strength and rise to the occasion to lead a terrific life ahead, with confidence and grandeur.

YOUR SUCCESS BOOKLET

(Don't forget to grab this!)

This booklet includes:

- 9 things that successful people are different from the mediocre
- 15 things successful people say no to
- 8 Steps to achieve anything you want in life

Get yourself mentally equipped before the journey starts.

To receive your success booklet, visit the link:

https://beausuccess.activehosted.com/f/1

REFERENCES

10 reasons you might find it hard to say "no." (n.d.). Blog.Speak-First.Com. https://blog.speak-first.com/10-reasons-you-might-find-it-hard-to-say-no

Barth, D. (2016, January 15). Why Is It Hard to Say "No" and How Can You Get Better at It? Psychology Today. https://www.psychologytoday.com/us/blog/the-couch/201601/why-is-it-hard-say-no-and-how-can-you-get-better-it

Clinic Staff, M. (n.d.). Stress relief: When and how to say no. Mayo Clinic. https://www.mayoclinic.org/healthy-lifestyle/stress-management/in-depth/stress-relief/art-20044494

Cy, S. (2018, July 25). How to Say NO Without Feeling Guilty, Mean, or Selfish. Medium. https://medium.com/the-mission/how-to-say-no-with-joy-and-conviction-and-without-feeling-guilty-mean-or-selfish-c7fd3f09711e

Dellitt, J. (2017, August 15). Real Talk: Why You Should Say "No" More Often. The Everygirl. https://theeverygirl.com/why-you-should-say-no-more-often/

Facts & Statistics | Anxiety and Depression Association of America, ADAA. (2000). Adaa.Org. https://adaa.org/about-adaa/press-room/facts-statistics

Hurst, K. (2017, November 21). How To Say No Without Feeling Guilty Or Being Rude. The Law Of Attraction. https://www.thelawofattraction.com/say-no-without-feeling-guilty/

Jacobson, S. (2015, March 24). The Psychological Cost of Never Saying No. Harley TherapyTM Blog. https://www.harleytherapy.co.uk/counselling/saying-no.htm

Sack M.D., D. (2016, October 17). 8 Ways to Stop Worrying About What Other People Think. Psychology Today. https://www.psychologytoday.com/us/blog/where-science-meets-the-steps/201610/8-ways-stop-worrying-about-what-other-people-think

Schweet, C. (2019, January 25). Why Saying No Is Difficult to Do | Carley Schweet. Self-Care for the Modern Mama. https://carleyschweet.com/why-saying-no-is-difficult/

Shanks, N. (2014, August 13). Ultimate Guide on How to Not Care What Other People Think. Nia Shanks. https://www.niashanks.com/guide-not-care-what-people-think/

Sidney Sadeghi. (2015, December 5). 6 Rules of Pain and Pleasure – The Science Behind All Human Action. Titanium Success; Titanium Success. https://titaniumsuccess.com/6-rules-of-pain-and-pleasure/

Suicide. (2018, August 24). Who.Int; World Health Organization: WHO. https://www.who.int/news-room/fact-sheets/detail/suicide

Ambady, N., LaPlante, D., Nguyen, T., Rosenthal, R., Chaumeton, N., & Levinson, W. (2002). Surgeons' tone of voice: A clue to malpractice history. Surgery, 132(1), 5–9. https://doi.org/10.1067/msy.2002.124733

Tartakovsky, M. (2018, October 8). 5 Boundaries That Actually Bolster Your Bond in Your Marriage. Psychcentral.Com. https://psychcentral.com/lib/5-boundaries-that-actually-bolster-your-bond-in-your-marriage/

Woznicki, S. (2020, January 3). 5 Powerful Mental Shifts to Stop Worrying About What Other People Think. Tiny Buddha. https://tinybuddha.com/blog/5-powerful-mindset-shifts-to-stop-worrying-about-what-other-people-think/

www.ingramcontent.com/pod-product-compliance
Lightning Source LLC
Chambersburg PA
CBHW020909080526
44589CB00011B/508